HOW
POETS
WORK

HOW POETS WORK

EDITED BY
Tony Curtis

seren

seren is the imprint of
Poetry Wales Press Ltd,
Wyndham Street, Bridgend
Mid Glamorgan, Wales

A CIP record for this book is available at the
British Library Cataloguing in Publication Data Office

ISBN 1-85411-131-0

*The publisher acknowledges the financial support of the
Arts Council of Wales*

Printed in Plantin by
WBC Book Manufacturers, Bridgend

Contents

Introduction
The Life of the Poem

This book introduces the reader to ten poets who talk about their view of poetry and share some of the mysteries of the art. These distinguished writers from England, Ireland, Scotland and Wales and the U.S.A. explain the practical issues raised by their working practices and make clear the importance of poetry in their lives.

Poetry is a form of writing which aims not to simplify as a scientific equation might be said to do, but rather to create a form of words which allows for and even encourages multiple meanings from multiple readings. Too often in an educational context the poem is treated as an encoded discourse which the student is challenged to decode and classify in some way. The poem may appear "obscure", a system of language signs and structures which are not reader friendly, a closed discourse in some way élitist and privileged. In *How Poets Work* some of our leading poets illuminate in a clear, honest and entertaining way the fascinations of their art. Poems rarely appear in a finished, pristine form; they have to be worked for. Like the craft of shaping; there are mistakes, revisions and re-workings; these are fully represented in *How Poets Work* by the inclusion of sample drafts of many poems.

I believe that poetry is born from some of the most necessary impulses that we have; and that, by its very nature, it distinguishes itself above and beyond all other forms of writing; and that the writing and reading of poetry takes a place at the very centre of civilised human life. As Anne Stevenson says, poetry's function "is to bring one's mind to bear so strongly upon reality that its false or fanciful appearances wither away" (page 47).

What are poems for? From what need are they born? For most people, most of the time, poems are a resource to be used at times of stress or celebration. They are the form of words one turns to at funerals, for marking special occasions, for expressing awkward feelings — on Valentine's Day, on birthdays, on passing one's driving test. "Poems" in these contexts manifest themselves as verse, and we may not want to consider them as poems at all. They are neat, short; they rhyme; they may tinkle or roll along with a predictable rhythm; they may establish and then subvert in a dramatic or humorous way the expectation of the reader or listener.

Such things have a useful, but strictly limited function. They are cars with engines, but no gears, with steering wheels, but flat tyres.

We sit in them like children at the fair, turning the false wheel to no
effect, for we are on ratchets, with rubber wheels that are destined
to go round in a fixed pattern. Safe as houses, solid as a rock, just
like clockwork. The clichés click like a clock.

I want to look at two poems, one by the American Theodore
Roethke, 'My Papa's Waltz' and one by myself, 'Spring fed'.

My Papa's Waltz

The whiskey on your breath
Could make a small boy dizzy;
But I hung on like death:
Such waltzing was not easy.

We romped until the pans
Slid from the kitchen shelf;
My mother's countenance
Could not unfrown itself.

The hand that held my wrist
Was battered on one knuckle;
At every step you missed
My right ear scraped a buckle.

You beat time on my head
With a palm caked hard by dirt
Then waltzed me off to bed
Still clinging to your shirt.

This poem has an obvious pattern of lines which alternate six
syllables and seven syllables — first a line with three iambs and then
one with an extra beat. It is arranged in quatrains which rhyme abab.
Nothing could be more orthodox, predictable, if you like, than such
a form. There is an obvious reason for this: a poem about a waltz is
surely enhanced by such a waltz-like system of beats and stresses.
'My Papa's Waltz' has all these things in common with the sort of
occasion verse which we would not wish to spend time on. However,
Theodore Roethke is not simply describing a dance; he is consciously using the undemanding form to carry deeply demanding
ideas and emotions.

The effect of the father's dancing, drunk in the kitchen, with his
young son, rather than his wife; her helpless observation of the
clumsy and destructive act; this larger than life, kitchen-size scene,
is powerfully saddening. It is so economically and precisely

recreated by Roethke's imagination and memory, for we naturally
assume that the speaker is the poet in this case: the knuckle, the belt
buckle, the understated clattering chaos of the pans, the whole
threatening, implied violence of the scene both undercut and height-
ened by the pathos of the son's clinging to his father. What else
should he do? Like many good poems, 'My Papa's Waltz' raises
questions which readers are challenged to answer from their own
lives.

My poem 'Spring fed' is, at first sight, quite different, in form and
theme.

Spring fed

the stone basin
fills and fills
from the swivel tap's
trickle.

The hills have shed
so much snow
and now,
the first brown grasses
clear of it,
the heifers push
up into the fields
to take the early shoots.

And it comes
again
the whole slow
turning of the season —
the softer touch of air,
the shine on the bucket,
the unclenching of things,
the lapping of water

in the stone basin
up to the rim,
and the very first,
this
delicious overspilling
onto our boots.

It's a thin poem which tries to emulate water trickling downwards.
There is no pattern of rhythm, but rhymes occur, sporadically.

Whereas Theodore Roethke's poem was clearly informed by personal experience, 'Spring fed' is cool, detached, an observer's witness of a moment in a farm dairy or outhouse in Spring. Or, more precisely, at one of those moments when Spring might be said to have arrived. How do we time the seasons? How do they announce themselves? Not by a single manifestation, not simply by a letter to *The Times* claiming a first sighting or sounding of the cuckoo. And, of course, that is what my poem attempts to do. A season creeps up on you, slips alongside your life.

But there is another dimension, for the conceit of the poem is driven by its voyeurism: the scene is really a painting by Andrew Wyeth, whose skill with tempura has created the illusion of wetness, so that the viewer almost feels as if his feet will get wet. Thus, a poem about the Winter-stored water which Spring releases is just as surely about the impressions stored by the artist on the canvas.

That poem was written in the 1980s and became part of a sequence of poems inspired by the paintings of Andrew Wyeth, possibly the finest living painter in America, and the son of the N.C. Wyeth whose illustrations for *Kidnapped* and *The Last of the Mohicans* played an important part in bringing narrative alive for this century's first generation of children. In one sense such poetry can work as a critique of the artist and his art; but I hope that these painting-inspired poems also live in their own right.

Poems may come from the work of other artists in other forms; poems may come from newspaper stories or features; poems may be suggested by overheard conversations, from landscape, music, or the sounds of a city. It can record, celebrate and tell stories. The poem can speak or act in voices other than those of the poet. We have been given a legacy of personal revelation by the English Romantic poets; we assume that the English lyric poem is always voiced by the poet himself. The painting 'Spring fed' is by Andrew Wyeth, but this response is that of Tony Curtis, because his name is underneath the poem in the Tate Gallery anthology *Voices from the Gallery*. This personal involvement can prove a burden on the poet and put blinkers on the reader. Later I shall show that a poet can speak in other tongues. But let me first examine the role of the poet's life.

In order to sustain the life and variety of the poem most poets extend themselves into areas of risk. Must they venture with their lives into extremes? Certainly, Coleridge would not have reached Xanadu without a dose of opium in his secluded Exmoor cottage in 1797. And wasn't Dylan the wild Welshman fuelled by loud pints of ale and swigged whiskies bought, always, by others? There is a natural curiosity to fill and flesh out the lives of the poets; we want these magicians to be distinguished by their actions, the visionaries to pay the price of their privilege.

But T.S. Eliot was a publisher's editor, Wallace Stevens, the insurance executive; Ted Hughes, the Devon farmer. Poets often go disguised as respectable people. You see, it's their minds that run riot and then tidy up the leavings. As Anne Stevenson says, "Trust the poem, forget the poet" (page 46).

'Inspiration' is a poem I wrote about the wild and practised bohemian artist Augustus John. At the beginning of this century John was an undistinguished student of art at the Slade School. On a vacation visit to his birthplace of Tenby, he took a dip.

Inspiration

The brain is bathed in blood — Dannie Abse

Was it Dorelia's breasts under a loose blouse?
Ida's ninth-month child-cavern of a stomach?
Caitlin's cataract of hair?

The princess' Indian Herb offered in the salon?
The sweet reek of a gypsy fire
under a fresh, split rabbit?

The smoky music light of Montmartre?
The dip and rise of the ballroom
as the famous danced over the ocean?

Or this —
a dive off Giltar Point into cool sea
that plunged him through seaweed
to butt the hidden rock.

Staggering back with the flap
of his scalp held in one bloody hand,
laughing out loud,

the sting of salt
throwing his head back to the red sky
and the jeering gulls,

his feet pressed firmly
into the mortal sway
of the wet sand.

On his return to London and the Slade, head bound up in a turban of a bandage, Augustus was lionised as the strikingly original young man that he himself began to believe in. My poem argues that the Pembrokeshire coastline knocked some sense into him; that the bohemian excesses of free love with the gypsies and the marijuana-parties of his rich friends were all desperate attempts to capture vision; and it argues that such visions might be as well accessed by the sea's hidden sharpness and the sweep of a Pembrokeshire beach.

On that summer night in 1797 when Samuel Taylor Coleridge was awakened suddenly from his visionary drug-dream by the infamous "person on business from Porlock" the true origin of his vision, he admits, was a book by Samuel Purchas, published in 1613. Falling asleep while reading *Purchas His Pilgrimage* Coleridge's mind played variations on that theme of the "Stately Palace" of Cublai Can with its "sixteen miles of plane ground with a wall, wherein are fertile Meddowes, pleasant springs, delightful Streams, and all sorts of beasts of chase and game, and in the middest thereof a sumptuous house of pleasure, which may be removed from place to place." Purchas's Xamdu becomes Xanadu, for rhythmic reasons; but more interestingly, Coleridge's poem goes on to explore the nature of imagination, for the poem ends:

> A damsel with a dulcimer
> In a vision once I saw:
>
> It was an Abyssinian maid,
> And on her dulcimer she played,
> Singing of Mount Abora.
> Could I revive within me,
>
> Her symphony and song,
> To such a deep delight 'twould win me,
> That with music loud and long,
> I would build that dome in the air,
> That sunny dome! those caves of ice!
> And all who heard should see them there,
>
> And all should cry, Beware! Beware!
> His flashing eyes, his floating hair!
> Weave a circle round him thrice,
> And close your eyes with holy dread,
> For he on honey-dew hath fed,
> And drunk the milk of Paradise.

What Coleridge is really interested in is the role of the poet in recovering and recreating the essence of such visions. We access the imagination in a meaningful way only by using language. We share with others our knowledge of the world and its material and ethereal being only through language. Poetry, as the most intense manifestation of language, is the most intense experience of the world which we can record and consider. Beyond the adrenaline flood of victory, beyond the high tide of orgasm, poetry is the wave we ride for a period limited only by our own mortality. Poetry itself is often concerned with mortality and the frustrations of the temporal.

Poems, like other art forms, are capable of manipulating time and they can affect our sense of the mortal life lived. Let me use as an example, my own poem 'Reg Webb'. Here is the final version, followed by a selection of the drafts from which it developed.

Reg Webb

had sailed the five oceans
putting out from Cardiff, Singapore, Boston,
he'd cork-screwed merchantmen
through icy shoals of Atlantic U-boats, then
in peace, piloted the fat oil hulks through
the maze of the Haven's rocky green and blue,
with their confusion of pipes to nuzzle
and suckle the Milford terminals.

Reg, landlocked for years in an armchair
in front of the tv's babble, stared
at his chipboard fire-place, the china,
chintz and brass, the gaudy gilt mirror.
Awash with bile, incontinent, bilges leaking,
his eyes watery and vast, was past pottering
with the roses and bulbs of the flat's
flower border, and shooing away cats.

Reg, becalmed in the straits of morphine
captaining his bed, full-sheeted, trim,
away from the port of his front room and tv,
the photo at the Palace for his O.B.E.
floundering and sick of being ill,
sank angrily, far out in the cottage hospital.
He's lost now, with fire in the hold, and a hard stroke
for one last evasive action, making smoke.

(1.)

Reg Webb

who had sailed three oceans
putting out from Cardiff, Singapore, Cape Town

who had cork-screwed revolutions through
any shoals of Atlantic U-boats too,
who plated the flat oil tanks in
the split embroidered redness green
with their confusion of pipes to supply
and nobble the Milford terminals.

Reg, landlocked in a armchair for years
in front of the tv's babble, before

the chiffoned electric fire-place, the china
chintzy and brass, the gaudy gilt mirror
awash with bile, incontinent, bilge looking
his eyes watery and red, part patterning
with the ones and halter of the flats
roseope strips of flowers hatches following the cats.

Reg, becalmed in the streets of maritime
captaining his bed, full-decked, trim,
away from the port of his closed front room and t.v.
this slot at the Palace for the O.B.E.
floundering and sick of being ill
sunk anyhow in the cottage hospital
for out

grudded at out out

and now my bit by

and now erosih onto, why ache.
one last

and now, fire in the hill, a hill other.
from other erosive actions making smoke

and now, fire in the hill, a hill other.

Reg Webb

who had sailed three oceans
putting out from Cardiff, Singapore, Cape Town

who had cork-screwed merchantmen through
icy shoals of Atlantic U-boats too,

in peace, piloted the fat oil hulks in
the maze of the Haven's rocky green,

with their confusion of pipes to nuzzle
and suckle the Milford terminals.

Reg, landlocked in an armchair for years
in front of the tv's babble, stares

at his chipboard fire-place, the china,
chintz and brass, the gaudy gilt mirror.

Awash with bile, incontinent, bilges leaking,
his eyes watery and vast, was past pottering

with the roses and bulbs of the flat's
flower border, and shooing away cats.

Reg, becalmed in the straits of morphine
captaining his bed, full-sheeted, trim,

away from the port of his front room and tv,
the photo at the Palace for his O.B.E.

framed
floundering and sick of being ill,
sank angrily, far out in the cottage hospital,

is lost now, with fire in the hold, and a hard stoke
for one last evasive action, making smoke.

As you can see from the first draft, it was started on February 19th, 1989. I was in Scotland to read my poetry at the St Andrews Arts Festival. It was very cold and snow threatened to wipe out the game of golf I had promised myself on the famous course. I felt beleaguered in my guest house. Phoning home to my wife and children I learnt that the old man who lived in the flat across from my parents in Pembrokeshire had died.

I should say that my relationship with Reg Webb was a fairly casual one. Also that I had not really learned as much about his life as I felt he had to share. Nevertheless, on that dismal afternoon in St Andrews I began to scribble ideas and memories to pull together what I felt his life had represented for me.

As you can see, the scribbles are roughly formed into the notion of poetry lines from the very beginning. I began writing while at University in 1965, so the poem is being written with twenty-five years of experience behind it. When school pupils ask me how long a particular poem took, I always answer, "Twenty-five years". People who write poems become poets when their writing comes out primarily, even naturally, as poetry rather than prose. By this, I mean not only that the quality of the language, the imagery, the rhythms, is rendered distinct from everyday speech, but that the language produced by the poet's thoughts and feelings derives its flow and pace from being spaced and measured into lines. Of course, what the poet aims for and what the reader expects is that distinctive shape of words, usually a rectangle of print in a sea of white paper. Poems announce their distinction, their otherness from prose by that seeming waste of paper. Publishers do poetry a great disservice when they cram poems in twos and threes onto the pages of collections and anthologies. The reader's eye needs to take a walk around a poem before entering it.

Of course, that typographical, visual distinction does not mean that poems may not do some of the work of prose, or fiction. What is clear immediately in 'Reg Webb' is that the writing is a narrative: I am taking what I know, adding to it what I can easily imagine, and then putting the whole down in a chronological order. There may be times when the writer decides to change the order of events in real time as an effective way of dealing with feelings and ideas, and of presenting these to readers in an intriguing and challenging way. I choose to be conventional in this poem; it is, after all, and from its very conception, an elegy, a piece in memory and praise of a dead person. In Wales such poems of praise and elegies are at the very heart of our tradition in both languages. The poet of a community, or bard, is the keeper of the keys of collective memory; the historian and story-teller.

When readers see poetry it is, of course, always in a finished, published state. However, there are very few poems in any language which emerge from the writer in such a polished form. Being a writer means constantly re-writing and shaping the early shapes and orderings of words into what one eventually determines to be the best form. Poems are never finished, only abandoned; so pronounced Ezra Pound, stealing the notion from the French poet, Mallarmé. There is a truth in that notion. Poets, in a sense, need to exhaust their energy and interest and commitment to a piece before finally sending it out to find its way and, hopefully, some readers in the world. This elegy is focused on the central fact of Reg Webb's life — his involvement with the sea, man and boy, in war and peacetime; this man works on the sea, with the sea. In retirement and old age these memories, though rarely articulated, seem to me to both sustain him and pain him in the years of physical deterioration and claustrophobic horizons.

From the three draft pages of 'Reg Webb' the progress of the poem may be followed from initial scribble to the third draft's changes of lines. And, importantly, the beginning of the realisation that the rhyming couplets form could well be better "hidden" in a larger structure of these verses or poetry paragraphs. It is in this third paragraph that I make serious efforts to rhyme the ends of lines.

Of course, as I have argued, all poetry does not have to rhyme: sometimes rhyme would distract from other aspects of the writing; sometimes it would seem inappropriate to the subject matter or language of the poem. When these inappropriate rhymes occur it can be for humorous or satirical purposes. In this poem I have no such motives. I want to remember and honour the man; at the same time I don't want to create too perfect and neat a pattern. At its end I want to convey a sense of frustration, of my not knowing the whole story.

In the first draft, written on the back of a folded memo, the working title is 'Reg' and it runs on into the first line. That first line is a cliché —

> ... who sailed the seven seas

and is immediately changed to "3 oceans". The lines appear to be roughly measured, with four stressed words. Even by the second fold of the paper the lines seem to be coupled. The final lines also form rhyming couplets —

tv / O.B.E.
ill / hospital

From the beginning then, and less than an hour after the phone call
had told me of Reg Webb's death, his elegy, because it was always
conceived as an elegy, is suggesting a form and structure.

The third draft is still hand-written and that indicates that I was
working on the poem over the three days of my stay in Scotland.
The rhymes emerging in the first draft are now a clear organising
principle. The poem is shaping itself in rhyming couplets. But those
two lines drawn across the page after the eighth and sixteenth lines
are an indication and query. I am counting lines and seeing the
possibility of forming three blocks of lines, or verses, whilst retaining
the rhyming couplets.

In draft five the poem is safely home on the word processor in my
study in Wales. It's essential that one works on typed and processed
poems. It is the only accurate way to measure your lines and make
informed judgements: Shakespeare could not have written his sonnets without a counting and measuring machine — it was called the
iambic pentameter. That ten syllable, five stress line —

Shall I compare thee to a summer's day?

was an infallible measure of the poet's art for centuries before IBM.
Many contemporary poets, often turning their backs on metrical
measures, have to rely on speech rhythms as they face the keyboard
and screen.

Between drafts three and five of 'Reg Webb' I seem to have
resolved the problem of the poem's ending. The ambiguity of the
war-time smoke-screen and the deceased's crematorium departure has
an ironical timing which I hope serves to resolve the poem's narrative while retaining the sadness felt at a life not fully shared or
remembranced.

From draft six onwards the poem assumes its final three-verse
shape. The poem from that point in the drafts is close to the form
and the language of its final "abandonment"; further workings are
a fine tuning. As Seamus Heaney has said of Yeats: "He proves that
deliberation can be so intensified that it becomes synonymous with
inspiration".

'Reg Webb' was first offered to the public on a visit I made to my
old school, Greenhill in Tenby, later in 1989, in the Spring. The
landscape of the poem was familiar to those students. I gave a copy
to Reg's widow, with some nervousness; however, she seemed

pleased that his life and character was to be preserved in that way. I think it is important for poets to talk to their community or constituency. Poetry should be a discourse which we can share with those who are not necessarily "poetic" or "poetry lovers" — that awful, patronising term which one still hears in use. I want poems to do work in the "real" world, the world of "telegrams and anger", as W.B. Yeats put it.

On February 20th, 1989 the snow which had flurried and settled over the town and golf courses of St Andrews melted away just as quickly. The poetry reading which I gave that evening with the Scottish poet Edwin Morgan was, therefore, actually attended by an audience. The Old Course at St Andrews put into perspective any smugness which I might have been feeling about having begun another poem. I lost three balls.

Dannie Abse has talked about the need which poets have to fill in the time between the sometimes long, sometimes impatient wait for the next poem. All the poet can do, he says, is to be prepared for the poem, to remain alive to the possibility of the new poem. I think that poets need to write reviews or teach, or practise medicine or stamp books or handle accounts, or play golf as strategies of preparedness and recreation.

Also, if poetry does not live in the world of sport and traffic and television and train tickets, it risks ossification. Of course, there is a special constituency — there are poetry societies, poetry magazines, and poetry readings; but I welcome the inclusion of poems in daily newspapers — *The Guardian* and *The Independent,* BBC television's "Closedown" poems, and the "poems on the Underground" scheme in London.

The Welsh Arts Council, in the 1970s, even introduced a "Dial-a-Poem" scheme using the then recently-introduced telephone recorded message system. Now when you phone the Cardiff poet Peter Finch, he performs a poem for you before apologising for his absence and inviting you to leave a message. I wonder how many poems he gets in response. When Sue Lawley condemns people to her Radio 4 Desert Island, the discs are an illuminating choice, but the Bible and Shakespeare are always given. These two rich veins of ore and poetry are under the surface of everything. During the 1980s, when I was Chairman of the Welsh Academy of Writers, we discussed various ways of presenting poetry to a new audience. The poster poem was an obvious one, but we even considered a poem beer-mat, sponsored by Brains Brewery!

Sometimes the feeling that poems reach too small and select an audience leads to frustration and a strident shouting — the poetry and jazz events of the 1950s, the pub readings that began in the sixties; "Poems and Pints" on HTV in the seventies and the "Performance Poetry" of the 1980s and 90s. The trouble is that too often it is difficult to distinguish the poetry from the performance, whether it be Rasta dub — "Consternation thru tha Nation," or the "poet" covering himself in cling-film and poking through a hole for the sake of letting necessary oxygen in and unnecessary ranting, formless words, out. That is not a fanciful notion: it forms part of the "act" of a Cardiff "performance poet".

Of course, such nonsense is of little significance. We shall see; and, of course, we shall not see. There is, however, a real dilemma here: the poem has two lives — through the eye and on the page and through the ear when it is voiced by the writer or more commonly the reader. It is tempting to stand up and shout about your work. Poetry, like Shakespeare's plays, comes alive when it is sounded. Listening to a poem is, essentially, taking a sounding of its effect and meaning. What you hear is what you get. Written poetry is at least as old as Homer; poetry as a structured, rhythmic device as old as the first community. When a community settles down and wishes to construct a shared idea of itself, then it needs to collectively remembrance, to hold the past for use in the present. Without that, there can be no predicted future, no civilisation. Chants, rhymes and patterns of sounds assist memory and involve participants. Such sounds sway bodies and animate feelings. The idea is shared, voiced, personal. Written language further facilitates and strengthens the products of that basic, essential civilising impulse. Why do preachers and teachers and politicians use the triplet, the first, second and third instance of everything? Why do we perform for and with our children the Hickory, Dickory Dock, Itsy-Bitsy Spider litanies of the nursery? Language is the most powerful tool we have, and when we successfully work to shape it, the patterns we make guide us on our way and catch us when we might fall. Poems are the sharpest focus, the most potent cocktail of the words we share.

I believe that poetry is the highest expression of our language: if we deny that early-rooted and human-defining need, then we shall live prosaically. As Donald Hall says: "Poetry is talk altered into art, speech slowed down and attended to, words arranged for the reader who contracts to read them for their whole heft of association and noise" (*The Unsayable Said*, Copper Canyon Press, 1994).

Poetry, by its very nature, does not go in a straight, unbroken line, and it may sometimes appear not to be pragmatic; it *foregrounds* language; and those very effects which make it poetry, which distinguish it from ordinary prose, from ordinary speech, can, at times, seem to get in the way of clear narrative and argument. Words are always freighted with meaning. But the reader who despairs at such nit-picking, such apparent detours and indulgences, the sort of novel reader who perhaps skips over the boring descriptive bits, can always be challenged to explain or show how the most effective of poems might have been expressed in any other way. When Dylan Thomas writes:

> Do not go gentle into that good night
> Rage, rage against the dying of the light

The apparently ungrammatical "gentle", the G and R alternate sounds, the rhyming couplet and the underlying template of the iambic pentameter, that ghost which haunts the entire body of classic English Poetry, these qualities are fundamentally lost in a prose rendition which reduces those lines to something like, "We really ought to make the most of our lives and live every moment as if it were our last". Or, "Life's a bitch, so shake your fist".

The meaning of poetry is essentially bound up in its form. Poetry is a superior form of expression to all prose forms of language because it adds to the sentence and paragraph that powerful device of the line: it is the line-break, the unjustified right-hand margin which distinguishes poetry from all the other uses of written language. In poetry the line is the unit of significance as well as the sentence, and the tension between these two controls allows the poet to control the fourth dimension of time. Presenting the reader with sentences which are cut into lines is the means by which the poet scores musical sounds. Only poetry touches the parts that prose cannot reach. Donald Hill again: "Poems tell stories; poems recount ideas; but poems embody feeling. Because emotion is illogical — in logic opposites cannot both be true; in the life of feeling, we love and hate together — the poem exists to say the unsayable" (*ibid.*).

Technique is the key, but too often in education we dissect the rat and are then surprised to find that it does not run back into the maze. We should always keep in mind the need to engage with literary texts through the emotions, before bringing our intellect to bear on them. Words must first move the heart, then move the brain. As Robert Lowell said, "Poetry is not the record of an event: it is an event."

But, however skilled and concerned poets are to encode the

feelings and ideas which motivate the poems, they can never be sure that anything of their original purpose will survive. In a sense, we all write to make something of ourselves survive, but what grows out of that effort may fail in its purpose, or be failed by the fact that its audience and context has shifted. I tried to suggest this in a prose poem which acted as a coda to my 1983 collection *Letting Go*.

Tortoise

They bought you a tortoise and every Autumn your father packed it away in its Winter box of straw in the house-loft. One year in the late Spring, you climbed up to find the box empty.

You all searched the grimy space, finding nothing and coming down dirty as sweeps. Years later, your mother writes that four houses further along the terrace they've found a shell in the loft. Just that. A shell, hard, perfect and whole. Inside, a shrunk ball of jelly.

The image makes you shiver for days, then it lodges in the back of your mind. To travel and come to nothing, leaving behind something shaped, hard and scoured out; an object which no longer holds or needs you, being finished, and what it was always growing towards.

Whatever you pack away neatly and safely may still move away from you in time; what you grow may be seen and used as something quite other by those generations which follow. The works of the Academicians are stacked, facing the wall or each other in the basements of our museums. The poetry which sang and flew for one age may lie in unopened books in the library stacks of a later age. Despite this obvious uncertainty, poems continue to appear and women (increasingly so) and men continue to aspire to the life of the poet. Broadly speaking, poets work for two reasons: firstly, they are motivated by the need to record and consider their own experience of life; and secondly, they address their society and times, raising questions about political and social issues. My interview with Lawrence Ferlinghetti exemplifies this political role. Some poets achieve poems in which the personal and public concerns intersect in striking ways. So often in this century the individual feels and seems adrift in a complex of political and economic forces which they seem incapable of directly affecting. The great, big poems — Milton's 'Paradise Lost', Wordsworth's 'The Prelude', Coleridge's 'The Rhyme of the Ancient Mariner' — have addressed humanity's

place in a firmament and a cosmos which is destined, or pre-des-
tined and which the poet, or his protagonist, heroically strives to
render palpable and significant.

In our century there have been notable poems in which the large
issues are raised. W.B. Yeats in 'Easter 1916' acknowledges that in
the Dublin revolt against British rule "A terrible beauty is born".
His role as a poet of national fervour was to create the climate out
of which the Easter Rising in Dublin was born. In one of his last
poems, 'The Man and the Echo', he wonders, "Did that play of
mine send out / Certain men the English shot?" Certainly, the
influence of the Irish writers in supporting the uprising against the
English was significant.

Yeats and T.S. Eliot, whose *The Waste Land* and *Four Quartets*
are the major poetic achievement of the century in English poetry,
have played an important part in shaping perceptions of our times,
and historians, thinkers, and articulate commentators will time and
again be drawn to quotations from such works. Shelley may have
been exaggerating when he claimed that "Poets are the unacknow-
ledged legislators of the world", but it is clear that it is in poems that
we find the means of articulating our deepest concerns. The Great
War, for example, now seems to be defined by the poems of Wilfred
Owen. In talking of such poets and poems, what I am doing is
constructing an argument which recognises the role of the modern
poet as bard. The outstanding poets are outstanding because they
offer insight into the workings of the real world by rendering their
experience of it into forms of words which create a different reality.

But what of W.H. Auden's famous, and worrying dictum, "Poetry
makes nothing happen"? Are "bards" to be nothing more than tired
old men in strange robes? Auden was the most prominent of those
angry, modern young men of the 1930s who were thrilled by the
machines of their age, but at the same time were anxiously observing
the fascist nightmare working its way through Europe. If such a poet
at such a time could express such quaking concerns, then what role
might one claim for poetry in the world of barbed wire and empty
soup bowls?

In the early 1980s I struck a chord with the poetry editor of *The
New Yorker*. Howard Moss published three poems of mine in 1981
and 1982. That most sophisticated and influential magazine, with
its advertisements for Cartier and Cadillac, published 'Land Army
Photographs', 'Tannenbaum' and 'Ivy': these poems, respectively,
deal with the way in which history contrived to place my father and
mother in the same area of Pembrokeshire in 1944; the ritual of

dressing the domestic Christmas tree; and lastly, how my ten-year-old son tried to help me to cut ivy away from an old pear tree in our garden. Here's my extract from 'Ivy':

> As we axed and ripped the tentacles,
> it slacked its biceps, unclenched its fist.
> I climbed and hacked while you
> dragged great clumps of ivy to your bonfire ...
>
> By October, winds should have scattered the dead leaves
> and you'll watch me climb again to snap
> the final twists of brittle tendril.
>
> At full stretch I shall prise them loose,
> then feed them down through the bare branches.
> And you, my boy, will look up to me with impatience,
> like a climber at the bottom waiting for ropes.

I want to argue that even that domestic poem, enacting as it does an incident of father / son contact and sharing can work to change the world. Imagine, it is Washington D.C. and a White House or Pentagon Master of the Universe waits for his dental check-up. He flicks through the *New Yorker*; has he time to start the short story? How about one of the two or three poems? 'Ivy' takes that person's mind out of the closed hub of the important things in life — the sweet, sore blisters of garden work, the musty smell of dusty creepers. It works to put things into a sane and proper perspective.

In 1995 I published *War Voices*, a collection of my poems about war from the last twenty-five years. Born in 1946 and growing up in the sixties and seventies, I have had no direct experience of war. But from the Dinky Toy battles on our front room carpet to the televised witness of Vietnam, the Falklands, the Gulf and Bosnia, I have lived alongside the other, safe side of warfare all my life. Helen Dunmore, in this book, explains how her television witness led her to a Gulf War poem, while Lawrence Ferlinghetti has some angry points to make about the role of television in such conflicts. As a sometime historian I know that the history of my family and all the people I know is the history of the two world wars. Educated, comfortable, the least I can do is research and rehearse some of those experiences.

At the end of last year, I discovered that my family had lost someone in battle. I had thought that all the men in my background worked in protected occupations. They were mostly farmers or railway workers, or quarrymen — then a distant relative gave me

the official death notice of James Charles Thomas, Private in the
Machine Gun Corps, my grandmother's cousin. Somewhere, sometime between November 30th 1917 and January 19th 1918 some
corner of France became forever Pembrokeshire. Someone should
remember that: I am ready to receive that poem when it wants to
come forward. And I can almost taste it. Precious are the
moments when personal experiences and associations intersect with
the shared poetic narrative that we call History.

When I have been asked to contribute a poem or small group of
poems to an anthology or radio programme, it is always 'Soup'
which I choose. Taken from a small incident in *Another Generation*,
Elie Wiesel's autobiography, in which he describes being a teenager
in Auschwitz, this imagined narrative within a monologue does not
mention the time or place. That way it can work as a specific
projection from that Polish axle-tree of Jewish suffering, but also
resonate with all the suffering camps in all the countries throughout
our botched world and century. It shows that to survive you need
two things — soup (whatever you have boiled in whatever water you
have), and the knowledge of who you are, who your people are. Of
course, to secure the one, you may risk the other.

Soup

One night our block leader set a competition:
two bowls of soup to the best teller of a tale.
The whole evening the hut filled with words —
tales from the old countries
of wolves and children
potions and love-sick herders
stupid woodsmen and crafty villagers.
Apple-blossom snowed from blue skies,
orphans discovered themselves royal.
Tales of greed and heroes and cunning survival,
soldiers of the Empires, the Church, the Reich.

And when they turned to me
I could not speak,
sunk in the horror of that place,
my throat a corridor of bones, my eyes
and nostrils clogged with self-pity.
'Speak,' they said, 'everyone has a story to tell.'
And so I closed my eyes and said:
I have no hunger for your bowls of soup, you see
I have just risen from the Shabbat meal —
my father has filled our glasses with wine,

bread has been broken, the maid has served fish.
Grandfather has sung, tears in his eyes, the old songs.
My mother holds her glass by the stem, lifts
it to her mouth, the red glow reflecting on her throat.
I go to her side and she kisses me for bed.
My grandfather's kiss is rough and soft like an apricot.
The sheets on my bed are crisp and flat
like the leaves of a book ...

I carried my prizes back to my bunk: one bowl
I hid, the other I stirred
and smelt a long time, so long
that it filled the cauldron of my head,
drowning a family of memories.

Poets work to prepare for poems like that. Poems which sound a truth, define a moment. At such moments "the brain is bathed in blood", the poet leaves self and becomes no more than an instrument for the sounding of poetry. You should be no less; and cannot be more. Poets may look and behave no differently from other people as they move through the world, but beware, there is a wildness there —

He holds him with his glittering eye —
The Wedding-Guest stood still,
And listens like a three years' child:
The Mariner hath his will.

The Wedding-Guest sat on a stone;
He cannot choose but hear;
And thus spake on that ancient man,
The bright-eyed Mariner.

Like the Mariner, I thank you for listening to me; though, of course, you had no choice.

Tony Curtis

Dannie Abse
The Ass and the Green Thing

1

In February 1946, when I was a twenty-two-year-old wide-eyed, poetry-writing medical student walking the groaning wards of Westminster Hospital in London, I would hesitate sometimes at the bed of a white-faced patient convalescing from major surgery. We had intermittent conversations about Sartre, Camus and Existentialism. And yes, he would quote Kierkegaard: "Terror, perdition, annihilation dwell next door to every man". We also discussed the Slow Rate of Demobilisation, the Character of Aneurin Bevan, the Rarity of Post-War Bananas. One afternoon I confessed to him that I wrote poetry and, at once, he advised me to send my verse to Hutchinson.

"They're on the look-out for new young poets," he told me.

Apparently my patient had vague connections with the publishing world and was privy to all kinds of secrets. He assured me that Hutchinson wished to cash in on the wartime boom in poetry sales. In those austere days of powdered egg, spam, and paper shortage, books of poems had been bought and read avidly by lonely, far-away-from-home Service men and women. Hutchinson, incompetent as ever, had missed out on such sales and now, compounding their commercial error, did not realise that the wartime boom was soon to be superseded by a peace-time plop.

Over the previous two years I had written more than thirty poems. I had called one 'The Yellow Bird'. Perhaps that could be the title of my neophyte volume? Alun Lewis's younger sister, Mair, reminded me, though, how Alun had taken his title *Ha! Ha! Among the Trumpets* from the Book of Job. I remember how I re-read Job seeking out a different title and soon I came across the ass that "searcheth after every green thing". *After Every Green Thing*. Would any critic spot the source of my self-deprecating title? But first, of course, Hutchinson had to accept my manuscript which I posted off, wishing it the best of luck as I pushed the big envelope into the red pillar box.

Months of silence. Then, in June, 1946, I was invited to visit Hutchinson's editorial offices to meet a certain Mrs Webb. I combed my hair, rode a bus and sat in an outer waiting room until summoned. Mrs Webb explained to me that they were in a quandary. My book had been sent out to two readers. One declared it to be utter bosh, the other that it was of "exceptional quality". I liked that — *exceptional quality*! As for the fellow naming it utter bosh well that was ... utter tosh! Mrs Webb, a Solomon if ever there was one, now pronounced that she would send my manuscript to a third reader. "It will depend on that report," she said, dismissing me. In September, 1946, I received a letter from Hutchinson accepting *After Every Green Thing*. It was more than two years before the book was actually published — for, meanwhile, Hutchinson had slowly come to realise that verse was no longer a commercial enterprise. And when, finally, it did reach the bookshops I continued to be deluded: I still thought the book had exceptional quality. Several years passed before I realised that half of it was bosh, and most of the other half tosh. Only then did I recall Aesop's fly, sitting on the axle of a chariot, that cried out, "What a dust I do make!".

Recently, because I was putting together a *Selected Poems* for Penguin Books, I took down *After Every Green Thing* from my bookshelf to see if I could choose at least one or two early poems for the Penguin selection. The majority were too flawed. Being untutored, reading Medicine, not English, unaware of literary criticism, mixing with students who owned no knowledge or theories about the craft of poetry, I had made elementary mistakes. Some of these I might have avoided had someone pointed me towards the Don'ts of Ezra Pound. Politically evil that American poet might have been but he had climbed Parnassus and come down with a tablet of stone on which the Muse had writ some vital commandments for the apprentice poet. These included:

> Go in fear of abstraction.
> Don't babble worn out poetic expressions such as
>   "dove-grey hills" or "pearl-pale".
> Don't mop up the particular decorative vocabulary of
>   some one or two poets whom you admire.
> Don't use such an expression as "dim lands of peace".
>   It mixes an abstraction, "peace" with the concrete
>   "lands".

I, the youthful author of *After Every Green Thing* did not go in fear of abstraction. Worse, the controlled explosion of a poem was too often triggered by a poetic idea rather than a true or imagined experience.

I fear, too, that I frequently babbled poetic expressions — not "dove-grey hills" exactly but a too liberal use of overworked poetic words: "stars", "wounds", "golden", "dazzling", "brilliant" etc. To write a poem is rather like inviting guests to a banquet. Only the guests are words. The banquet is only a success if the right guests come, if the host places the correct guests next to each other. It is no use placing "blue" next to "sky" — they have talked too much to each other; like "lonely" and "heart" they have nothing more to say. It is a risk to ask "wound" and "blood" to the feast because they are tired guests; they have been overworked these last years. They are liable to fall asleep before the meal is through.

As for mopping up someone else's decorative vocabulary I had caught totally the inflated hortatory tone of the then fashionable neo-romantic poets whose work could be found pervasively in the poetry magazines then available and which I compulsively read: *Poetry Quarterly, Poetry London, Outposts*. Rhetoric was the order of the day. Of course there were gifted poets in the 1940s, not least those who had been killed in the war — Keith Douglas, Alun Lewis, Sidney Keyes. And Dylan Thomas, above all, managed to make a genuine and thrilling poetry out of his rhetorical energy. But there were many other poets, the vast majority in fact, who, in the pages of such magazines as *Poetry Quarterly* merely offered "poems" that owned an ornamental emptiness and were crippled mortally by a florid profuseness of language.

Middleton Murry once remarked how rhetoric was the opposite of crystallisation, how "instead of defining and making concrete your thought, by the aid of your sensuous perception you give way to a mere verbal exaggeration of your feeling or your thought. Instead of trying to make your expression more precise and true, you falsify it for the sake of a vague impressiveness ... You try to replace quality by quantity and forget that all quantities raised to an infinite power are the same. By pounding on the keys with a hammer you merely break the strings". The "You" Middleton Murry was addressing could have been the "Me" of *After Every Green Thing*.

Sometimes I caught more than the organ vatic tones of those *Poetry Quarterly* rhetoricians. Nor did I escape the influence of the master neo-romantic himself — Dylan Thomas. Thus a phallic and soma poem of mine, 'The Marriage' begins:

> Once no morning could make quiet his spires
> his chapels and chimneys blasphemed the golden day;
> when choirs of wounds arose from the sunken bed
> arose the hairy hand of Esau which slept in his face
> and the book of children shut in his head.

And concludes:

> For the bird of his guilt no longer aspires
> to leave the cages of the golden day:
> her mouth is his wine and her breasts are his bread
> and wings are tied by chains to a yesterday.
> Now she dies in his eyes with the mortal dead.

Imprecision of language, words chosen more for sound than sense and, if all that was not enough of elementary error, here I was doing what Pound had imperiously said Don't do — mixing, as in "bird of his guilt", an abstraction (guilt) with a concrete object (bird). Many other poems in *After Every Green Thing* were scarred in this way. Now, turning over its pages, I seek and I find "delicious domes of possibility", "ark of loving", "panic of a blank page", "private desert of insanity", "slippers of darkness", "white pain of the moon", "pharaoh of summer", "mountains of dark", "security of armchairs", "a monastery of tears". How easy it is to make up such expressions. Anybody half-literate can construct them. Some may appear more arresting than others and major poets might on occasions present one such (for instance, Wordsworth's "Fields of Sleep") but, generally, as a poetic strategy, it is too easy an option and to write good poetry one must be committed to difficulty.

Sometimes, as an apprentice poet, in trying to avoid clichés and seeking a reaction of surprise, I forgot that the best word in context, like the best image, the best stanza, had not only to be surprising but appropriate. For example, I wrote in one poem, "They with thoughts like gods in their muscles". Surprising yes, a cliché no, but since thoughts are never like gods in muscles the expression is inappropriate, almost absurd. Images devised only to startle lose their small effervescence on a second reading to become utterly flat — boring as an anecdote told over and over. Thus a surrealistic mode of poetry, depending on strange conjunctions, on odd gestures of surprise — rather like somebody coming out from behind a curtain and shouting "Boo" — is bound ultimately to fail. Such poetry worships the Arbitrary, that false idol. Poetry, to be authentic, must allow the reader an *illusion* of inevitability however decorative its logic.

So many flawed poems then in that first youthful book of mine. It would have been useful if somebody with a greater literary sophistication than I possessed had listed these and other faults and, in so doing, speeded up my rather prolonged apprenticeship. On the other hand, I would not wish to suggest that a tutorless apprenticeship had no advantages or proved to be entirely barren. After all, the two most original poets of the 1940s, Dylan Thomas and George Barker, did not even go to University. Being a medical student allowed me entrance, painful entrance, to experiences that would have been missed had I merely read sweet English at Oxford or Cambridge. Besides, though over the years my poetry has become more conversationally pitched, more linguistically economical and, I hope, more authentic, appropriate, I find occasions, when the poem itself, in its development, *insists* on a singing tone. Then a neo-romantic mode reasserts itself — the Dionysian material, however, now partly tamed and shaped by Apollonian decorum. Indeed, soon after *After Every Green Thing* was published I wrote an Epithalamion of which I am still proud:

> Singing, today I married my white girl
> beautiful in a barley field.
> Green on thy finger a grass blade curled,
> so with this ring I thee wed, I thee wed,
> and send our love to the loveless world
> of all the living and all the dead.
>
> Now, no more than vulnerable human,
> we, more than one, less than two,
> are nearly ourselves in a barley field —
> and only love is the rent that's due
> though the bailiffs of time return anew
> to all the living but not the dead.
>
> Shipwrecked, the sun sinks down harbours
> of a sky, unloads its liquid cargoes
> of marigolds,and I and my white girl
> lie still in the barley — who else wishes
> to speak, what more can be said
> by all the living against all the dead?
>
> Come then all you wedding guests:
> green ghost of trees, gold of barley,
> you blackbird priests in the field,
> you wind that shakes the pansy head
> fluttering on a stalk like a butterfly;
> come the living and come the dead.
>
> Listen flowers, birds, winds, worlds,
> tell all today that I married
> more than a white girl in the barley —

for today I took to my human bed
flower and bird and wind and world,
and all the living and all the dead.

2

I had begun to write poetry when I was a sixth form schoolboy living
in a politically conscious household — one of my brothers, Leo,
would become a Labour Member of Parliament. Like him I hoped
to change the world! For it seemed to me then, briefly at least, that
a sacred indignation could touch one into a spontaneous eloquence.
I thought, along with Wilfred Owen, that the poetry was in the pity
and that the poetry did not matter. Thus the first "raw" poems I
wrote, those antecedent to the much more private artefacts in *After
Every Green Thing*, had a missionary intention. I sympathised with
George Herbert when, on his deathbed, I learnt that he had
suggested his poems, *The Temple*, should only be published if they
would do good. Herbert was not concerned whether his poetry
would give pleasure or not, and as such he was a typically committed
poet, albeit in his case not politically but religiously committed. His
poetry, he felt, was only valuable if it were effective as God's
propaganda. His intention was to bring despairing human beings
nearer to God.

A year or two passed before I became aware how much committed
fervour could be accompanied by humourless intolerance. I read
Henry Vaughan's seventeenth century hectoring introduction to
Silex Scintillans with mounting irritation. "That this kingdom,"
thundered Vaughan, "hath abounded with those ingenious persons,
which in the late notion are termed Wits is too well known; many
of them having cast away all their fair portion of time in no better
employments than a deliberate search, or excogitation, of idle
words, and a most vain, insatiable, desire to be reputed poets ... And
well it were for them, if those willingly studied and wilfully published
vanities could defile no spirits but their own; but the case is far
worse. These vipers survive their parents and for many ages after
(like epidemic diseases) infect whole generations, corrupting always
and unhallowing the best-gifted souls and the most capable vessels ...".

Despite my political concern, anger, about — as I put it — "slums
and cripples in a world of colours" — I felt sympathy for the
brotherhood and sisterhood of Vaughan's vipers. I began to understand that missionary public poetry was of no greater significance
than any other kind of poetry. No more, no less. British poets,

particularly in our modern times, usually depreciate the activist value of their writings, however much their work is infused with moral concerns. They find it difficult to believe that literature, and poetry in particular, is important in the "great world" other than allowing readers perdurable pleasure. Stephen Spender asked despairingly, "What can we do in a world at war that matters?" and Auden asserted, "Poetry makes nothing happen", recognising that he merely belonged to a tribe of dreaming things.

> What canst thou do, or all thy tribe
> To the great world? Thou art a dreaming thing.

So wrote Keats looking in the mirror. On the other hand, poets of our time, those who have lived in totalitarian societies, have found that to be a dreaming thing can be lethal. Consider the unenviable fate of so many European poets, some of whom hardly wrote public poetry at all. Mayakovsky committing suicide, Mandelstam jumping through a window of a Soviet hospital, Garcia Lorca murdered, Hernandez dying of T.B. in one of Franco's dark dungeons, Paul Celan and Primo Levi enduringly wounded though surviving Nazi concentration camps, Brecht and Milosz and Brodsky exiled — and so on.

It would appear that totalitarian governments believe poetry to be a subversive weapon whatever poets themselves might think. Poems politically coloured may not have the immediacy of certain television images but some may set off detonations into the future. For if we accept that ideas in themselves can change us, can direct us into a different life-style, how much more powerfully can ordered imaginative experiences, by which I mean poems, affect us, influence us and through us change society at large?

But I am arguing with myself! I merely wish to signify how my poetry moved from platform verse towards work that did not strive to change the world. Indeed, many of the poems in *After Every Green Thing* were too private. Jung, in an essay 'Psychology and Literature' remarked that "the personal aspect is a limitation — and even a sin — in the realm of art. When a form of art is primarily personal it deserves to be treated as if it were a neurosis". If Jung had substituted the word "private" for "personal" then I would be able to agree with him. Paradoxically, the private with its tendency to become hermetic — as, for example, in the work of John Ashbery in the U.S.A. or of Medbh McGuckian in Northern Ireland, is perceived by the reader to be impersonal with any feeling in it, at best, muffled.

Of course, a poet with a missionary intention, a platform poet attempting to address a large audience, may feel his vocation to be worthwhile, one that is socially purposeful. Others, primarily writing with no audience in mind, avoiding hermeticism, committed only to making the best poem they can with the gift they have, may, in certain desolate moody moments, wonder whether their occupation and preoccupation with language in a society that thinks in Prose, is simply a self-indulgence, even a symptom only of a neurotic personality. Sometimes, I confess, I have, in my maturity, asked myself this question. I find solace in two lines from a poem I wrote called 'Funland':

> Love, read this, though it has little meaning
> for by reading this you give me meaning.

3

Through long experience of trying to write poetry I believe I have become an expert in "Don'ts". I can advise an apprentice poet on what not to do; but I can't tell him or her how to write a poem. I myself do not know how to write the next poem, though I can trace how I wrote verses in the past, their origins and linguistic strategies. For poetry, as I have said elsewhere, is written in the brain but the brain is bathed in blood. Or, as Shelley put it, "Poetry is not like reasoning, a power to be exerted according to the determination of the will. A man cannot say, 'I will compose poetry'. The greatest poet even cannot say it; for the mind in creation is as a fading coal, which some invisible influence, like an inconstant wind awakens to transitory brightness; the power arises from within, like the colour of a flame which fades as it is developed, and the conscious portions of our nature are unprophetic of its approach or its departure."

We can, though, be *prepared* to write the next poem. "Chance favours the prepared mind," declared Louis Pasteur. What is the nature of that chance? I remarked earlier that when I began writing the controlled explosion of a poem was triggered by a poetic idea rather than by a true or imagined experience. But it is better to write from experiences for these, dramatised, in any case frequently encapsulate an idea. In brief, if one writes truthfully some truth emerges. And yet the arrival of a sudden experience, or the summoning up of a potent memory, is rarely the whole story of a poem's source. Poems have — if I may use medical jargon — a multifactorial aetiology.

Let me trace the origin of a modest poem of mine, one that did
not have a too complex genesis, an autobiographical piece called
'Portrait of the Artist as a Middle-Aged Man'. One morning I
received a letter from a stranger about a poem in *After Every Green
Thing*. I was taken aback. After all, more than twenty years had
passed since the publication of that flawed book; besides, only five
hundred copies of it had been published so, fortunately, it had found
few readers. Nevertheless here, evidently, was one misguided
reader. He seemed to be keen on the following lines:

> It is enough to endure the thief in the clock
> and the apple-flesh turning brown after the bite;
> it would be enough to see our first shy loves
> passing us by, hand in hand, with their strange
>   sad children.

My reader should not have been admiring of, "the thief in the clock"
— such a cliché; but the image of the apple-stump turning brown,
well that, I decided, was fine. Indeed, the more I thought about it
the more I liked it. I liked it because the image was *authentic*: the
apple-flesh does turn brown after the bite. I liked it because the
image was *commonplace*, not exotic — everybody knows how the
apple changes colour. I liked it because, despite being commonplace, it was not a cliché. In fact, I have never read one single poem
in which this familiar image featured.

Some days after I had responded to my reader's letter I tried to
write a poem in which I used the image of an apple tarnishing. The
poem failed. After a few drafts I gave up. Months passed before I
attempted to work on a new poem. This time the poem was wrecked
by the insertion of the apple image. The next poem, too, met a
similar fate because of my need to use this same image from *After
Every Green Thing*.

Christmas came and went and then, early in the New Year, I wrote
'Portrait of the Artist as a Middle-Aged Man' — twelve autobiographical lines:

> Pure Xmas card below — street under snow,
> under lamplight. My children curl asleep,
> my wife also moans from depths too deep
> with all her shutters closed and half her life.
> And I? I, sober now, come down the stairs
> to eat an apple, to taste the snow in it,
> to switch the light on at the maudlin time.

Habitual living room, where the apple-flesh
turns brown after the bite, oh half my life
has gone to pot. And, now, too tired for sleep,
I count up the Xmas cards childishly,
assessing, *Jesus*, how many friends I've got.

My favoured image, as you can see, had drifted into a brief poem
which dramatised a small suburban *experience* — of a middle-aged,
married protagonist who, on New Year's Eve, had become maudlin
— perhaps earlier had drunk too much and sung Should Auld
Acquaintance! — and then, in the middle of the night, unable to
sleep, had glanced out of the bedroom window at the snow-lit
ground before descending the stairs to the living room. There he
eats an apple as he observes the Christmas cards on the mantelpiece.

It is a situation, I would suggest, that is easily believable. The
poem owned, at the very least, or so I judged, fictional truth: a winter
apple when bitten can taste cold; winter on January 1st at 3 a.m.
may find the ground covered with snow; Christmas cards often
decorate a living room and quite a number of people, as I soon
discovered after I finished the poem, count up their Christmas
cards! In short, the situation and experience, would be acceptable
to the reader being universal enough.

So the poem's genesis was powered by both an image and an
experience. The experience, as I've speculated, seemed believable
enough but why did I think that the apple image had now found an
apt context? It felt right to me but I only became convinced it was
right when I began to ask myself what this poem, this anecdote in
twelve lines, was about. I thought of the snow outside, how it had
come into the apple within the living room; how the snow outside,
especially in towns, soon becomes tarnished with brown marks in
it, not unlike the apple-flesh itself that does so with the passing of
time. Time. January 1st. And all the Past past. An anniversary that
makes the middle-aged think of "the thief in the clock". Has not the
poem something to do then with time passing and the loss of
innocence, the brown tarnishing of the pure snow-whiteness within
the apple? So I pondered and then it occurred to me. The apple
image was truly a just one for do we not associate the biting of an
apple with a loss of innocence? Eden, The Tree of Knowledge. I
can believe that some readers would question my post-poem critical
reasoning. It does not matter to me. I am merely trying to explain
why I am satisfied that the image of the apple turning brown has,
as far as I'm concerned, come home.

One further point. The experience I retailed could be true or simply imagined. Truth, as Whitehead once pronounced, "adds to interest"; but poetry finally becomes fiction even when it does not start as fiction. All poetry, confessional or otherwise, belongs to the non-fiction shelves of libraries and bookshops. The poet needs to tell believable lies — so much poetry is in the details — in order to utter truths.

4

Mozart, it is said, could hear a whole new symphony in his head before he recorded it. He could simply write it down mechanically rather like a secretary being dictated to. Beethoven, like most composers, had no such awesome facility, though no lesser a musician. He had to cross out and cross through, recover and revise his musical scores over and over. The majority of poets, too, Beethoven-like, need to work through multiple drafts fastidiously before they arrive at the final unabandoned poem.

Youthful readers are surprised that this should be so. Perhaps they recall how Keats once wrote that "if poetry comes not naturally as leaves to a tree it had better not come at all". Such readers imagine a poem will lose spontaneity if worked over and over. But a poem, generally, has to go through many rehearsals before curtain-up when, like a play on opening night, it should have the semblance of a spontaneous creation.

Quite recently I wrote a poem which I eventually called 'Cricket Ball' where I used the Apple-Eden image again, though not initially. If I look at the first draft, ignoring scratchings out and alterations, I discover I wrote a most unpromising thirteen lines. It was not even a grammatically correct note. It was short-hand prose in cut-up lines:

> When I was a boy watching Glamorgan
> Slogger Smart, No. 6 for Glamorgan,
> big hitter, that time they only gave him 6
> when the ball left the Arms Park
> into the Angel Hotel. Smashed a window,
> *The Western Mail* said. Newspapers lie.
>
> *The Western Mail* could have had a scoop.
> The mystery was the ball never landed.
> It went *over* the Angel Hotel, over the Castle wall
> on and on out of sight.
>
> I think it's flying still. I wait

at the Angel Hotel looking up at the
sky. The world is round, teacher said.

It is a wonder that I bothered to work on such a piece. True, I was
not put off by the absurd idea of a cricket ball circling the world,
possibly returning, if I waited outside the Angel Hotel long enough.
And the memory of Cyril Smart hitting the ball out of the Arms Park
when I was a boy gave me pleasure, of course, even as I retrieved
that memory. More encouraging, was that I suddenly knew the end
of the poem, if it developed properly: "I smell cut grass. I shine an
apple on my thigh". An apple, not a shining red cricket ball. Ten
drafts or so later the poem read:

As a minto-sucking boy
I watched Glamorgan play.
Slogger Smart, No.6, unrenowned,
burly Cyril, but the biggest hit with me.

One game he won single-handed.
I was there when, from the applauding ground
the ball flew high, higher
over Westgate Street
to smash, they said, an hotel window
— a discreet, Angel Hotel window.

Lies! *The South Wales Echo* missed a scoop:
THE BALL THAT NEVER LANDED.

Over the Angel it arched
a rainbow trajectory
high over the High Street
over Cardiff Castle walls
on and on out of sight
till out of sight it went on and on.

Cyril Smart, you never suffered
the disgrace of fame
but I remember, I was there:
a pre-war boy with an uplifted face —
else someone with my name.

Sometimes I fancy the ball may,
hell for leather, still be flying
round the turning world
to arrive back here one summer's day.

It's late. Cyril, poor light stopped your play.
I, too, peer at a failing sky
over Westgate Street.
I wait. I smell cut grass.
I shine an apple on my thigh.

So now 'Cricket Ball' had expanded to thirty-two lines. At least, it no longer offended grammatically, its syntax was straightforward and the sound of it unlike prose. This was partly the result of vowel orchestration, frank rhyming such as "discreet" and "Westgate Street", "unrenowned" and "applauding ground", "late" and "wait".

Some things still bothered me. Since I was not writing an elegy for Cyril Smart I should not focus on him late in the poem. So perhaps it would be best to excise "Cyril, poor light stopped your play". That expression, in any case, was somewhat defenceless, bathetic. The poem, above all, I decided, needed to be more economical, needed to be tightened up. I thought that by continuing to keep the sound of the meaning right it would not require too many revisions. But a further ten drafts followed before I arrived at a more economical penultimate version:

1933, I watched Glamorgan play
especially Hurricane Smart, unrenowned,
but the biggest hit with me.

A three-spring flash of willow,
WHAM,
and the thumped ball would leave
the applauding ground.

Once, hell for leather, it flew
over the workman's crane
in Westgate Street

to crash, they said, through a discreet
Angel Hotel windowpane.

But I, a pre-war boy,
(or someone with my name)
wanted it, that Eden day,
to mock physics and gravity,
to rainbow-arch the posh hotel
higher, deranged; on and on, allegro,
(the Taff a gleam of mercury below)

going, going, gone
towards the Caerphilly mountain range.

Vanishings! The years, too, gone like change.
The Taff flows but seems the same.
It's late. I peer at the failing sky
over Westgate Street
and wait. I smell cut grass.
I shine an apple on my thigh.

In the introductory note to my *Collected Poems 1948-1976* I confessed
how "for some time my ambition has been to write poems which
appear translucent but are in fact deceptions. I would have the
reader enter them, be deceived he could see through them like
sea-water, and be puzzled when he cannot quite touch bottom". To
be sure, the truly deceived do not realise they have been deceived,
so are not puzzled, imagining they have touched bottom. The poet
himself, in his best work, may not apprehend the poem's depths.
The best poems are more wise than the man or woman who made
them, more clever, more lyrical, more witty, more knowing, more
striated with feeling than the poet realises. No wonder Vernon
Watkins murmured to himself, "Trust darkness".

In writing poetry I have often attempted to define odours not quite
identifiable, to name something perceived momentarily in the
corner of the eye, to interpret a whisper just out of intelligible
earshot. In short, I have tried to engage with the mysteries. Yet
'Cricket Ball' can hardly be classified as embracing the ineffable.
It is more explicit than many other complex poems I have written.
And yet I hope it still may entrap the reader with undercurrents of
suggestion and feeling and something unsaid. Frankly, though, I
only chose 'Cricket Ball' to demonstrate the maturation of a poem
because I happened to have the working sheets at hand. In addition,
its thematic core (I nearly wrote apple-core) relates to the earlier
poem I quoted — 'Portrait of a Middle-Aged Man'.

After I thought I had finished 'Cricket Ball' I learned that Cyril
Smart had actually hit the cricket ball out of Cardiff Arms Park into
the Angel Hotel in 1935, not 1933. At first, I was loath to opt for
historical sporting accuracy if only because "1933" rhymes with
"the biggest hit with me". But then I recalled my phrase "the
disgrace of fame" so, by inserting it early in the poem, I could, by
the use of "free" — "free from the disgrace of fame" — re-establish
a simple rhyme. This would allow me to begin with "1935".

However, when a word is changed in a poem it often happens that

another word also requires alteration. It is a bit like plumbing. Mend
one leak and another springs up in the system elsewhere! Rhymes
themselves may suggest associations; for instance, "1935" and "a
cricket ball alive". Moreover, I allowed myself one more punning
device. Not like "gone like change" and "same" — but a frivolous
progression from "three-spring willow" to "the sound of summer".
Here's the final version:

> 1935, I watched Glamorgan play
> especially Slogger Smart, free
> from the disgrace of fame, unrenowned,
> but the biggest hit with me.
>
> A three-spring flash of willow
> and, suddenly, the sound of summer
> as the thumped ball, alive, would leave
> the applauding ground.
>
> Once, hell for leather, it curled
> over the workman's crane
> in Westgate Street
> to crash, they said, through a discreet
> Angel Hotel windowpane.
>
> But I, a pre-war boy,
> (or someone with my name)
> wanted it, that Eden day,
> to scoot around the turning world,
> to mock physics and gravity,
> to rainbow-arch the posh hotel
> higher, deranged, on and on, allegro,
> (the Taff a gleam of mercury below)
> going, going, gone
> towards the Caerphilly mountain range.
>
> Vanishings! The years, too, gone like change.
> But the travelling Taff seems the same.
> It's late. I peer at the failing sky
> over Westgate Street
> and wait. I smell cut grass.
> I shine an apple on my thigh.

So much fiddling with words, even for an inconsequential poem
such as this. No wonder Marianne Moore remarked of poetry,
"I, too, dislike it: there are things that are important beyond all this
fiddle". No wonder I also feel sometimes like the ass that searcheth
after every green thing. Not that the ass has a choice. Besides, as

Marianne Moore also wrote:

> I, too, dislike it
> Reading it, however, with a perfect contempt for it,
> one discovers in it after all, a place for the genuine.

Anne Stevenson
The Only Green in the Jungle

Once upon a time, in the late 1950s, I lived in Belfast. My English husband and I were in our twenties, and we liked to go to nightspots (or whatever drab equivalents Belfast offered) to drink and dance and pretend we were in New York. One night, we were sitting over lukewarm Martinis watching a floorshow when a tall rangey brunette in a clinging gown drifted into the spotlight and sang a song. "Love, love, love," she sang in a high, nasal whine, "love, love, love". I know now that it was (and is) quite a famous song, but it was new to me then. I remember nothing else about the evening, and little, really, about Belfast save that we lived far out on the Kilmarnock Road, next door to a happy-go-lucky Roman Catholic family whose children I sometimes harboured while their parents spent weekends in bed. How long we lived there, what had brought us there, even what my husband looked like — all the details are missing. Except for that refrain "love, love, love" and the tune that went with it.

A year later we were really living in New York. The notorious sixties were revving to take off, but I remained ignorant, unaware of emergent hippidom and flower-power until my marriage broke down (by then we were living in the deep south) and I returned to my roots in Ann Arbor. I enrolled for an MA degree at the University of Michigan, and under the tutelage of Donald Hall was soon in thrall to American poetry. When I next visited New York, I met only poets. One night, in a Greenwich village nightclub, a famous jazz trumpeter was performing. The tiny place fairly reeked of smoke and noise and sweat and sexual excitement. I don't remember if "Love, love, love" was on the programme, but I came away repeating two lines:

> As if love, love, love
> were the only green in the jungle.

The lines duly turned up, a little altered, at the end of a poem called 'New York'.

> This addiction!
> The ones who get drunk on it easily!
> The romantic, sad-hearted,
> expensive inhabitants
> who have to believe there is no way out,

who tear at themselves and each other
under the drumbeats while everyone
dances   or weeps
or takes off clothes hopefully,
half sure that the quivering bedstead
can bring forth leaves,
that love, love, love
is the only green in the jungle.

It's not easy to generalize about the way poets work, but the way in which "love, love, love" travelled from Belfast to New York and then spirited itself unexpectedly into that cadence says something about how, when I don't labour, poems sometimes work on me. Perhaps I was born with an extraordinary gift for self-deception, for as often as not, the arrival of a poem signals a wrong-turning. When writing 'New York', for example, I believed I'd had the time of my life. In a single week of "sin" in Bohemia, I had thrown away, I thought, a long heritage of accumulated puritanism. "Love, love, love."

So I wrote the poem, starting from the lines at the end, letting that "love, love, love" song provide the rhythm. When I'd finished — after some attempts, I recall, at a Whitman-like rhapsody — I realised that I had spiked my own balloon. It was no celebration of love that I'd produced but a poem of rueful mistrust. The luridly unnatural life of the city is judged to be an "addiction"; people thrive there by tearing themselves and each other to pieces. Peeling off their clothes, they are only "*half* sure that the quivering bedstead / can bring forth leaves ...". Where was my rhapsody? Was it that song, finally, that revealed its own fatuity? A sentimental song about phoney love, as I must long have sensed.

Had I been a scholar or a critic more self-consciously knowledge-able about literature, I might have seen through the irony of the poem into something of its lineage: in Propertius, in Chaucer, in Shakespeare's *Troilus and Cressida* where in Act III, Scene i, a tipsy Helen banters with Pandarus "Let thy song be love. This love will undo us all, O Cupid, Cupid, Cupid!" And Pandarus obliges, "Love, love, nothing but love, still love, still more!" On the other hand, had I been less naïve I might have hesitated to follow in such august footsteps. 'New York', slight as it is, was written at first hand. Even though famous precedents lay thick around it (such is the poet's apology), the *impulse* to write it was fresh. 'New York' turned out to be a poem of self-revelation.

After more than thirty years, 'New York' seems not inappropriate, either, to the mood of hopeful delusion that characterised the sixties.

That I can still trace the genesis of 'New York' must mean that it
somehow epitomises the occasion of its making. Trust the poem,
forget the poet. Except that for this poet, the making of even so
minor a poem helped cut through a confusing maze of emotions to
a small clearing in the wilderness.

I emphasise the personal sources of this poem because critics so
often gather a "text" to their bosoms while discarding the author.
On the other hand, ordinary readers, eager to savour "facts" about
a writer's *apparent* life, are inclined to ascribe over much to bio-
graphical details. Experience teaches me that, in the main, writing
poetry is an exploratory process, each poem a stage in what Yeats
called the poet's quarrel with himself — a quarrel, if you like,
between the imagination that sits down excited by words and the
critical mind (and ear) that pushes its findings further and further
in the direction of reality. Eliot called this confrontation the "intolerable wrestle / With words and meanings".

Before the flowering in this century of a ubiquitous and transcon-
tinental self-consciousness about language, the poet's "intolerable
wrestle" would not, I suspect, have been so generally acknowledged.
It used to be thought that to write, the poet had to be inspired. The
muse was an embodiment of nature ("Unless poetry comes to the
poet as naturally as leaves to the tree," wrote Keats, "it had better
not come at all") or an emissary from the gods. Remember Shakespeare's Jacques in *As You Like It* mockingly uniting the "The
lunatic, the lover, and the poet" who are "of imagination all com-
pact;" suggesting that each, in his way, is deceived, and imagination
causes the deception.

> The poet's eye, in a fine frenzy rolling,
> Doth glance from heaven to earth, to earth from heaven:
> And as imagination bodies forth
> The forms of things unknown, the poet's pen
> Turns them to shapes, and gives to airy nothing
> A local habitation and a name.

Such a view of the imagination, whether or not it was Shakespeare's own, called forth Eliot's frank exposition of his struggles
for precise meaning (not to name airy nothings, but to give substance to somethings) in the fifth section of 'East Coker':

> So here I am, in the middle way, having had twenty years —
> Twenty years largely wasted, the years of *l'entre deux guerres*
> Trying to learn to use words, and every attempt

Is a wholly new start, and a different kind of failure
Because one has only learnt to get the better of words
For the thing one no longer has to say, or the way in which
One is no longer disposed to say it. And so each venture
Is a new beginning, a raid on the inarticulate
With shabby equipment always deteriorating
In the general mess of imprecision of feeling ...

I grew up in the shadow of Eliot and Yeats, and the poets I first emulated were, on the whole, suspicious of the airy nothings of imagination's deceptions. I tended to look critically at Keats's inspiration and Coleridge's "shaping spirit". An impatient scholar, I worked out a poetic for myself. One function of imagination (I thought) is to create a state of mind that offers an alternative to reality (often a more acceptable or spiritual alternative); both poet and reader can subscribe to it, in Coleridge's words, by "suspending disbelief". Another function, more apposite to twentieth century investigations into the nature of language, is to bring one's mind to bear so strongly upon reality that its false or fanciful appearances wither away. What remains cannot be called the "truth" because, as Eliot eloquently demonstrated, "the fight to recover what has been lost / And found and lost again and again" never finishes.

So it happened that when I really began to write, around about 1961, the process was already an exercise in trial and revision. I still affirm that one of the chief functions of poetry, the more so in a world dominated by advertising and media-speak, is to sharpen language, to demonstrate by example that language, however imperfect as a vehicle of truth, can at least expose its own susceptibility to misuse. And yet, without "inspiration" and flights of imagination, how can poetry exist? How will it come into being as a form of spontaneous expression beyond, as it were, the limits of language? This was not, of course, a question I consciously put to myself; only from a distance can I see that it split me in two.

That paradox and contradiction often prove fruitful is a characteristic of poetry that distinguishes it from prose. The poet has to rely upon instinct to break through logic, and instinct appears to be a mixture of acute awareness (particularly of speech-sounds) and sheer luck. Spontaneously a line will occur as if overheard. I write it down, on a notepad, usually, or on a scrap of paper. If the line or idea suggests a rhythm I try to fashion it into a sound-shape or stanza. It sometimes happens that a poem — a short poem, say, like 'New York' — writes itself almost by accident while I am trying to write something else.

At other times, "inspiration" is simply visual. Last April, for
example, I rose early and went downstairs for coffee. Out of a
window facing west into North Wales, I could see, at about a half
mile's distance, a shepherd on his scooter ferrying a black plastic
bag of silage up the stony road to his sheep. I am never in Wales
without being conscious of geological antiquity; of eroded mountains sliced and furrowed and gouged by glaciers departed only
yesterday, of the thinness of the soil and the precarious nature of
the life it supports. I had been searching (as I still search) for a way
of expressing the "feel" of contemporaneous age in that landscape.
A phrase or two occurred to me, and I scribbled them down, still
looking out the window:

> And then came the ice age, and then came
> Gwilym, a sack of silage balanced on his scooter
> mobbed by his flock. Each sailing ewe
> tugs along a white dinghy — but now
> some of the lambs have lost their mothers.
> They bound back helter-skelter over the rocks;
> brittle nickering answered by iron baas
> ~~I can't hear~~ I feel without hearing
> ~~like vibrations~~

Not very promising, but I found my notebook and tried again in the
space under a note made earlier in the week: "April's thin milky light
(in Wales) a change of season in it". My second version I titled 'In
Deep Time?'. Then I crossed it out as being too pretentious.
Nevertheless, the second version seemed more focused.

> ...Then came the ice age and then came
> Gwilym, a sack of silage balanced
> on his fell-scooter, mobbed by his flock.
> Each ewe in sail tugs its dinghy, but now
> some of the lambs have come unmoored.
> They bound back helter-skelter, the scraped rock
> must be ringing with brittle nickers and iron baas
> I don't hear for window glass between us
> and five hundred fifty million years.

My husband joined me for breakfast, after which I took up my
notebook again and saw immediately that the poem should begin
with the last line: "Five hundred fifty million years" (approximately
the age of the Cambrian rocks). I also realised that a "k" sound could
be repeated throughout: "flock" and "rock" could be joined by

"forked" instead of "balanced", "look" instead of "now" and the more accurate "unhooked" instead of "unmoored". "Nickers", an absurd homophone of "knickers", would have to go. There were many ice ages; if I substituted "glaciers" for "ice age" the guttural alliteration would sound well with "Gwilym". Mid-morning found me with the next-to-last draft:

> [First;] five hundred fifty million years,
>
> then came the glaciers,
>   and then came Gwilym,
> a sack of silage forked on his fell-scooter,
>   mobbed by his flock.
>
> Each ewe in sail tugs its dinghy
>   ... look,
> some of the lambs have come unhooked.
>
> They're bounding back helter-skelter,
>   the scraped rock
> must be ringing with brittle maas
>   and iron baas
> I don't hear for window-glass and
>
> April's thin milky light, Wales
> and all those winters [in it.]

When I showed the draft to my husband, he suggested that I omit "in it" (a hangover from my original note) and simply end with poem with "winters". I did that, and then cut out the initial "First", as unnecessary.

★

Years ago I went to hear Robert Frost reading his poetry in Ann Arbor. There were some poems he preferred not to dissect — he would just read them. Others he was pleased enough to take apart and put together again if the audience wished. I think of both 'New York' and 'History' (a tentative title for the Gwilym poem) as poems suitable for the dissecting table. While neither pretends to be more than an aside, I find them satisfactory to the ear, and they both suggest, I think, more than appears on their surfaces. Perhaps I should add that such poems — simple as they sound — do not come automatically. I am hardly a more competent poet today than I was thirty years ago. Each new poem offers a fresh challenge, and unless my ear takes it on (as, for instance, rhyming "fell-scooter" with "helter-skelter") my will can do nothing. A poem can take months, years, to find its right form. Sometimes, with luck, it can fall into shape in hours.

A long poem, say three to six pages, is always more difficult to achieve than a short one. I generally write longer poems in bits — a stanza here, a few lines there — before I get to grips with the whole. It is not unusual for me to begin a poem and then realise after some weeks that it's gone wrong, that it has nothing to do with the poem that is trying to write itself through me. Look, for example, at an attempt I forced from my pen two years ago, after I'd spent an afternoon taking notes in a tiny churchyard that surrounds the early Christian church at Llandanwg.

I had been trying for some time to write a ballad for Sion Phylip of the *Phylipiaid Ardudwy*, one of a family of poets who in the sixteenth and seventeenth centuries lived on nearby Mochras. According to legend, Sion Phylip was drowned in a shipwreck in 1600, travelling back to Mochras after a ceremonial recitation in Pwllheli. Welsh subjects always make difficulties for English-speakers, but I hoped to evade them by establishing a stanza and then breaking out of it — as it were, from strict "form" into informal musings about the nature of elegiac poetry. Little pleases me about this opening of a poem I never finished, but it may be of interest to see how it led me to a nursing home two hundred miles away in East Anglia.

> Anonymous sand is whistling around Bardd Phylip,
> Emptying and filling the pouches of his name.
> Proficient in genealogy and recitation,
> He drowned in 1600, wrecked off Lleyn.
> Of the eloquent breath and hum of him remain
> A slab of Cambrian grit, a curled inscription,
> The wind's illiterate pickings scouring it.

That might have been a promising opening (end rhymes are indicated) if it had not been such blatant pastiche. The drafts show that I next made a pretence of honesty.

> A bard's way to begin, I suppose. But
> this is not an elegy. I haven't the heart
> to stretch English rhymes around
> the pious scab of *Richard Owen, Gent,*
> in 1694 *departed this life in the 82nd*

year of his age. Equal in silence, one
Capt. Meyrick Ellis, late of Harlech,
dropped into Llandanwg's sand in 1907;
a widow and two daughters' chiselled loss.

> *My loving wife and children dear*
> *Mourn not for me as I sleep here.*
> *For I sleep here in hope to rise*
> *To life with you in Paradise.*

Well, they're in heaven, happily
gone to heaven. And if not, hadn't they —
as good or better — the illusion of it?

Hope lies among lies so restfully, Mary, while
there you are, locked out of Wales in your 82nd
year, a hyphen crying for a final digit.
You don't know even if our nonagenarian 19's
will see you though — 'through' not 'up'
dear Mary. Your salty principles still refuse
crack-pot superstitions ...

I wrote on in this vein for a stanza or two, though I knew there
could be no future for a poem that had taken itself right off the track.
What had begun as an elegy for the dead of Llandanwg had turned
a corner and become a poem — a more personal poem — about
Mary (my mother-in-law) in whose house I was living and on whose
table I was writing. Before I realised what was happening I'd
scrawled a title at the top of the first page: Visits to the Cemetery of
the Long Alive.

I looked at the title, doubted, got up and made a cup of tea, looked
again and closed my notebook. Next morning I put what I had of
the poem on the word processor to see what it looked like. Nothing
about it cohered. I went for a walk. I came back and wrote down
some isolated lines: "could you, though, take consolation in negative
bliss? / Not eternities of song and sugared angels / just painless,
everlasting release from rotting nails and puffy useless ankles /
tussles with the nurses, hours on the commode / the indignity of
shaving, balding, balancing massive breasts on a pigeon's chest ..."

The details mounted up and spilled over several sheets of ruled
paper. Abandoning that first draft altogether, I began again. The
poem had to be set in the nursing home.

As we might expect, a flat
generous lawn, two rows of cypresses —

> a little ragged these days; they can't
> afford a full-time gardener —
> a kitchen plot with stakes for runner beans,
> brambles along the wall (decrepit brick)
> ~~and a plum orchard.~~
> There must have been a biggish orchard,
> plums, apricots. Today around the trees,
> an all-purpose handyman is driving
> a noisy, unembarassed tractor-mower ...

After some weeks, a version existed of 'A Sepia Garden', but it was weeks before I showed a draft to my husband; and months before I thought it ready to send to Matt Simpson, who for some years has generously provided me with astringent pre-publication criticism.

Many drafts went into the completion of 'A Sepia Garden' — probably between twenty and thirty. It became the first poem of a sequence called 'Visits to the Cemetery of the Long Alive' in *Four and a Half Dancing Men* (1993). I never went back to the poem about Bardd Phylip and the Llandanwg churchyard, but its failure led me to something I had to finish. Here is the final version of the first stanza:

> Though you won't look at it,
> a flat, generous lawn;
> two rows of cypresses, ragged
> (these days such places can't afford
> a full-time gardener); kitchen plot
> with stakes for runner beans;
> brambles along a brick wall;
> and beyond the washing lines,
> a wild place with bearded trees
> that must have been an orchard.
> You can still pick plums there,
> and grey apricots, but today,
> pulping the windfalls,
> an all-purpose handy-man
> is driving a tractor-mower.
> Preceding us, he makes it easier
> to push you in your chair.

Revisions and refinements arrive through repetition, lines said aloud until the vowels and consonants flow naturally to the ear. Free verse is in this respect more difficult to test as being "right" or "wrong" than verses in traditional patterns, or those that establish their own schemata — as in the stanza that evolved in the Llandanwg churchyard. Thus far, this essay has cited poems in free verse, tested by reference to what could be called an inner ear. Mine, I believe, is still an American ear, modified through many years' residence in Britain. But I enjoy, too (in a sense, it's more fun) writing consciously in set forms, playing the game of verse, sometimes not seriously, sometimes seriously enough. Often such poems appear after I have immersed myself in other poetries.

For example, in the winter of 1992, I was asked to prepare a lecture for the University of Michigan — my American alma mater — on some aspect of literature related to "The Geography of Identity". I was not sure I had anything to say. "Identity" is one of those words that is freighted with emotion without carrying its fair share of precision. With a year in hand to complete the lecture, I decided to approach the subject by comparing some poems by the American, Wallace Stevens (whose views on poetry and imagination have long interested me) with others by Louis MacNeice and Robert Graves. I had also been asked to speak at a seminar in Swansea. I decided to give my Michigan lecture a trial run there, but when both universities asked for a title in advance, I was hard put to know what to give them. As I sat at my writing table one morning, pondering the Janus face of language, a line appeared and I wrote it down. "The way you say the world is what you get." I guessed it might be the title of one of Stevens's poems, but no. On second thought, it sounded more like Graves; the line was more cynical about language than Stevens would have been. But it wasn't Graves either, though it moved in perfect iambic pentameter — ten syllables, five stresses. What was the first line of Elizabeth Bishop's villanelle, 'One Art'? "The art of losing isn't hard to master."

Almost instantly, I knew that 'The Way You Say The World Is What You Get' would be both my title for the lecture and the first line of a villanelle. The poem got written long before the lecture and later proved useful to it. For, as poems will, it told me what I thought. The limitations of form became the hurdles on which my conscious mind trained while unconsciously I became aware of how much I *differed* from Stevens (whose aesthetic made few allowances for social pressures on language) and essentially agreed with Graves (who in his poem 'The Cool Web' argues that language is an element we contrive, not to reveal reality but to protect us from it).

As it turned out, 'The Way You Say The World Is What You Get' updated Graves by introducing a completely contemporary presence: the television. I had already written several poems on television's soul-devouring rapacities, so I was on familiar ground as I laid out several rhymes: *get, net, set, forget, it(?), jet, market, alphabet,* and so forth. As I needed a second rhyme, I provisionally noted down a second line "What's worse, you haven't time to change or choose". Choose gave me *lose, news, use, accuse, rose(?).* The rhythm, of course, rode its regular five stresses. As I look over my drafts I see that I marked out the pattern aba/ aba/ aba/ aba/ aba/ and the final quatrain abba. Once the grid was set, I could begin to fill it in.

> The way you say the world is what you get.
> What's more, you haven't time to change or choose.
> The words swarm (swim) out to pin you in their net
>
> Before you know you're in the TV set
> Stunned and strapped into the age's news.
> The mind's machine — and you invented it —
>
> Grinds out the formulas you have to fit,
> The ritual syllables you have to use
> To charm the world and not be crushed by it.
>
> This cluttered motorway, that screaming jet,
> Those crouching skeletons whose eyes accuse,
> Until you see the words you can (can't) forget..?
>
> That truth is wider (vaster) than the alphabet,
> Too horrible to find, too rare to lose ...

Here the draft breaks off. The poem was going awry. I must have left it for long enough to forget it. The next draft manages to push through to the quatrain, leaving the forth and fifth stanzas incomplete:

> Whichever way, you say the world you get,
> Though what is there is always there to lose.
> No living name can save the poisoned rose
> The absolute's irrelevant, and yet ...

The line "No living name can save the poisoned rose" was almost immediately revised to "No *crimson* name *preserves* the poisoned rose", "crimson" and "poison" chiming beautifully with each other. Later, after testing the poem in Swansea, I substituted "redeems" for "preserves". It was not until February of 1994, after the villanelle had appeared in *Poetry Review*, that I substituted "The" for "That" at the beginning of the fifth tercet; I had intended "That" to be a conjunction, but it read as a demonstrative pronoun, drawing too much attention to itself: not *that* world, but *the* world.

> The way you say the world is what you get.
> What's more, you haven't time to change or choose,
> The words swim out to pin you in their net
>
> Before you guess you're in the TV set
> Lit up and sizzling in unfriendly news.
> The mind's machine — and you invented it —
>
> Grinds out the formulae you have to fit,
> The ritual syllables you need to use
> To charm the world and not be crushed by it.
>
> This cluttered motorway, that screaming jet,
> Those crouching skeletons whose eyes accuse,
> O see and say them, make yourself forget
>
> The world is vaster than the alphabet,
> And profligate, and meaner than the muse.
> A bauble in the universe? Or shit?
>
> Whichever way, you say the world you get.
> Though what there is is always there to lose.
> No crimson name redeems the poisoned rose
> The absolute's irrelevant, and yet ...

After I had completed 'The Way You Say The World ...' (presently called 'Alas') I wrote no poetry for many months. I felt (I still feel) that the villanelle marks the end of a road I'd been following ever since 'New York' and the other poems of my first book, *Reversals*. The urgency to discover *at first hand* something of what people are, what love is, what history is, what language is, what nature is — an urgency that drove me into poetry (as it admittedly drove me into personal error) has in some important way dissipated. That Yeatsian quarrel with myself that produced poetry may, over thirty-odd years, have metamorphosed into a quarrel with the world which Yeats claimed only produces rhetoric. But that's not quite true either. I'm not sure that our quarrels can be so easily compartmentalised. What 'Alas' may have taught me is that my quarrel with myself has all along been a quarrel with the (human) world; or more precisely, that without "love, love, love" (the true, not the false variety) there is little to be said for human beings and the world their "alphabet" has so amazingly created, and which now, empowered by technology, it seems so blindly ready to destroy.

Visits to the Cemetery of the Long Absent

Anonymous sand is whistling around Bardd Phylib.
Emptying and filling the porches of his name,
Proficient in genealogy and recitation —
He drowned ~~circa~~ in 1600, wheeled off Lleyn,

~~Celebrated~~   Of the ~~turbulent claimed eloquent~~ breath and hum of their refrain
eloquent   A slab of Cambrian grit, a curled inscription,
A wind's illiterate pickings, — scouring it ...

A Bard's way to begin, I suppose, But
this is not an elegy. I haven't the heart
to ~~scratch~~ ~~trite~~ ~~scout~~ ~~scabrous~~ ~~facus scytch~~ rhymes around
the ~~first feeling~~ scab of Richard Owen Gent,
in
~~the~~ 1694, departed this life in the 82nd
year of his age. Equal in silence, here's
Capt. Meyrick Ellis, late of Harlech,
dropped into Llandanwg's sand in 1807;
a widow's and two daughters' chiselled loss.

Well, they're in heaven ~~by now~~, happily
gone to heaven. And if not, hadn't they —
as good a better — the illusion of it?
              My loving wife and children dear
              Mourn not for me as I sleep here.
              For I sleep here in hope to rise
              To life with you in Paradise.

Hope lies among lies so restfully. May, while
here you are, locked out of both in ~~your~~ the 82nd year of
crying for last digits, ~~with~~ a ~~starved~~ deprived your ~~tent~~ hyphen.
You don't know even if our nonagenarian
1900's will see you breathe — breathe, not up,
dear May; your salty principles still hate

crock-pot substitutes. I never knew
an atheist was atheist. Could you, though,

take consolation in negative bliss?
Not eternities of song and sugared angels,
just painless, everlasting release
from fungoid nails and puffy, useless ankles,
tussles with the nurses, hours on the commode,
indignities of shaving, balding, balancing
~~hotting~~ ~~heavy~~ tolls of ~~marbled~~ ~~breasts~~ on a pigeon's chest?

The wall is with you and without you,
as it shrivels away, about the size, how,
~~of an~~ neat 18 inch T.V. Screen you ~~slightly~~ ignore —
~~as the~~ ~~looming~~ ~~took you~~
~~In side~~ ~~that~~ ~~later, dispeller intimacy, you're useless~~
~~Keeping it~~ ~~vaguely~~ ~~because its there.~~
Letting it ~~chatter~~ slighter on because its there —
Where do we come from, ~~where~~ we ~~do~~ appear
in my ~~arms~~ ~~carrying~~ chocolate for ~~prawn~~ sandwiches ~~as flowers~~ ~~Suddenly~~ if here
to your,
a dahlias in cellophane, ~~to be~~ met with lamentation

Visits to the Cemetery of the Long Alive

Anonymous sand is whistling around Bardd Phylip,
emptying and filling the pouches of his name.
Proficient in geneology and recitation,
he was drowned, ~~since~~ 1600, wrecked off Lleyn.
Of the ~~perished~~ breath and hum of him remain
a slab of Cambrian grit, a curled inscription,
wind's illiterate pickings, scouring it.

A way to begin, I suppose. But
this is not an elegy. I haven't the heart
to stretch ~~new~~ rhymes around
the pious scab of Richard Owen, Gent,
in 1694 departed this life in the 82nd
year of his age. Equal in silence,
Capt. Meyrick Ellis, late of Harlech,
dropped into Llandanwg's sand in 1807;
a widow and two daughters' chiselled loss.

Well, they're in heaven ~~now~~, happily
gone to heaven. And if not, hadn't they -
as good or better - the illusion of it?

My loving wife and children dear
Mourn not for me as I sleep here.
For I sleep here in hope to rise
To life with you in Paradise.

Hope lies among lies ~~so~~ restfully, Mary, while
there you are, locked out of ~~Wales~~ in your 82nd year,
crying for last ~~digits like a begging hyphen~~.
You don't know, even, if our nonagenarian '19
will see you though - "through" not "up",
dear Mary; your ~~earthy~~ principles ~~oppose~~ all

You don't know, even, if an nonagenarian
1900's   will see you through ~ "through" and not "up"
dear Mary, your salty principles, steel . scary

"crock-pot" superstitions . I never knew
an atheist unaffected. Could you, though

take consolation in negative bliss?
Not eternities of song Sugared angels,
just painless , everlasting release
from toiling nails and puffy, useless ankles,
tussles with the menus, hours on the commode,
the indignity of shaving, balding, balancing
the uselessly morning breasts on a pigeon chest.

The world is with you and without you
as it shrinks away ~ about the size now / shrinks
of an 18 inch T.V. screen. "look, it
"I'm here, I love you." "I don't believe it
you mutter carefully "
carefully

"Is it really you?"
A hand extends whitely.
your   and we kiss it.

as we might expect, a flat
generous lawn, two rows of cypresses -
a little ragged these days; they can't
afford a full time gardiner —
a kitchen plot with stakes for runner beans,
brambles along the wall - (decrepit brick)
and a plum orchard.
There must have been ~~an~~ a bigish orchard,
plums, ~~and~~ apricots. Today around the trees
An all-purpose handyman is driving
a noisy, unembarrassed tractor-mower
not looking at us, but making it easier
to push you, ~~so following on his wake~~ in his wake.
                as
~~but~~ he sets off down a long corridor
between ~~two~~ beds, potentilla, buddleia, blue
jumped by a so musty lavender
~~But we~~ have to stop. Even you,
with your eyes slammed shut, smell it
begged you, ordering you to open up, ~~and take it~~
this ~~beauty~~
Here everything in a ~~little product of soul~~ sachet
you even died, two years
At last "They ~~are~~ allow you to pick it, you know."
He ~~would not pick~~ take a stalk, crushing it in
                                        unstidy ~~your~~ fingers

The scent is so strong it stings, your eyes water
as it crumbles into grey-blue ash;
about as much as we get - most of us,
saved for a while in a little gauze pouch
to throw away with our clothes -

Visits to the cemetery of the long alive

As we might expect, a flat
generous lawn, two rows of cypresses,
a little ragged/-- these days they can't
afford a full-time gardener --
a kitchen plot with stakes for runner beans,
brambles along the wall (decrepit brick)
and not far from the washing lines,
a wild place, with bearded fruit trees.
It must have been an orchard. You can still pick
plums there, and apricots.
But today, around the unloved trees,
an all-purpose handy man is driving
a noisy, unembarrassed tractor-mower, not
looking at us, but making it easier
to push you along his wake.

He burrs off, cutting a long green corridor
between old-fashioned beds - sages, potentillas,
fringed by so much bee-keeping blue lavender
we have to stop. Stop.
Even you, hunched like Welsh stone
with your eyes slammed shut, have to smell it
begging you, ordering you to remember.

Pick a stalk, crush it in your fingers.
It's scent is so strong it stings.
Your eyes water as it crumbles. into grey-blue ash.
About as much as we keep, most of us,
our by accident memories,
saved for a while in a little gauze pouch
to throw away with our clothes.

[handwritten:] Save it for a little while in a gauze pouch.
Then throw it away with our clothes.

[handwritten:] The common little worlds
p.... ma... life

6 verses

a a a
b a a
a a a
    —— a
a b a b
b { a { a
a   a   a
    ——   d

That comes out in yellow red &
                                blue

The way you say the word
      is what you get.

Whats worse, You haven't time to change of chance

without mind   So much we miss, So much
liberts or choose   yet?   we have to lose
    and choose   The Truth is vaster than the alphabet
    the you have to

                    (So much you say, So much you miss forget
                                                            forget

    Slang perdaction
    something & violence in   elements
    por perception   require
    terminology   the news
    by pretence

        Old story of a
                                    relevant
            Terminology is eminent

Phone Gerda - Hair, wed,
Mrs. Offers - Jigsaws...   extremist)
3 light bulbs   Sex
  Kalms   Soap, tooth paste,   Clues alone
    Bath
    plants   Mon.   Tuesday, John
    trains   1.10 - Yorks & Heleas   e bang
    wed.   Lunch
        Carrie   mary train -
    Check Trains to Bristol   9th launch
                                        (Hobby Easter)
        Phone Alan Wall   Motorway architecture
  C Black.   { the gimmick
                                the Sales push -

views chone · refuse muse
Cliens   accuse

let   The way you say the world is what you get,
                     And
          what's what, you haven't time to change or choose,
          The words swim out and pin you in their net,

          Before you know you're in the T.V set,   news
          You're stunned and stopped into the age's news,
          The mind-machine (and you invented it)

          Grounds out the   formulae   you have to fit,
          The internal syllables you need to use
          To   the word   and not be lost in it,
                                                        crushed by
          To   say   the word it   which you want to get
gimmicks   The home of glory   to make the world the world you can't to get
          The self go   to say the world the way you want . and get
                                        - - - forget

The jet   will not
                comment of hone -
the market
          5   The   to   - fenations of the (jet)
who sin
create the market   And how the market dries
of corrupted taste   The   -   the market and the - - -
                                Lies are a good as

4 lins   6   The home-toweb of the market
gadgets
gewgaws   The Huckster   with the market in his grip
market - speech   The market forces of the
media - speech

                           The cluttered motorway
                                The screaming jet -

The way you say the world is what you get,
~~truce~~ you ~~haven't time to change~~ choose
is not the words you're ~~sure~~
The words swarm out to pin you in their net,

Before you know, you're in the T.V. set,
stunned and shopped into the ~~gag's~~ news,
2   The mind's machine (and you invented it)
Grinds out the formulae you have to fit,
3   The refusal syllables you need to use
To charm the ~~truth~~ and not be crueled by it,
world

This cluttered motorway, that screaming jet,
~~those marching~~
~~That crowd of~~ skeletons whose eyes accuse —
4
Until you ~~slam~~ words you can't forget
see with
much larger than
That truth ~~is larger~~ that the alphabet,
5   Too humble to find, too rare to lose
~~and some matter~~
~~We have to make~~

And
~~of~~
what
~~King~~
is,

new invented
The ~~whole impacted~~
~~make a fuss~~
~~at great~~
with a wild regret

the   occluded
~~a~~ view ~~threaded~~ by
~~the faith~~ regret

~~Of what we make~~ ~~But totally what we get~~
~~you~~ ~~the spotless~~
~~Shut down~~ ~~the dreamed~~
the ~~untouched~~

Born   ~~By~~   its revolution
~~the resistance~~ and ~~the~~
1 what is,   oh
Experience   the let

the ~~handle~~ of
the ~~right~~ man and ~~the~~ miracle — oh let

The way you say the world be what you get

The way you say the world is what you get.
What's more, you haven't time to change or choose.
The ~~world swims~~ out to pin you in its net
   wide swarm
Before you guess you're in the TV set,
Lit up and sizzling in unfriendly news.
The mind's machine – and you invented it –

Grinds out the formulas you have to fit,
The ritual syllables you need to use
To charm the world and not be crushed by it.

This cluttered motorway, that screaming jet,
Those crouching skeletons whose eyes accuse;
O see and say them so you can forget

That world is vaster than the alphebet,
And profligate, and meaner than the muse.
A bauble in the universe?   Or shit?

Whichever way, you say the world you get.
Although what is is always there to lose.
crimson No ~~living~~ name ~~can save~~ the poisoned rose;
redeems The absolute's irrelevant.   And yet...

Alas

The way you say the world is what you get.
What's more, you haven't time to change or choose,
The words swim out to pin you in their net

Before you guess you're in the TV set
Lit up and sizzling in unfriendly news.
The mind's machine – and you invented it

Grinds out the formulas you have to fit,
The ritual syllables you need to use
To charm the world and not be crushed by it

This cluttered motorway, that screaming jet,
Those crouching skeletons whose eyes accuse,
Oh see and say them, make yourself forget

The world is vaster than the alphabet,
And profligate, and meaner than the mean
A bauble in the universe? Or shit?

Whichever way, you say the world you get.
Though what there is is always there to lose.
No crimson name redeems the poisoned rose
The absolute's irrelevant, and yet ....

Ex egi monumentum
aere perenius.

Anne Stevenson

Lawrence Ferlinghetti

Uses of Poetry

So what is the use of poetry these days
What use is it What good is it
these days and nights in the Age of Autogeddon
in which poetry is what has been paved over
to make a freeway for armies of the night
as in that palm paradiso just north of Nicaragua
where promises made in the plazas
will be betrayed in the back country
or in the so-green fields
of the Concord Naval Weapons Station
where armed trains run over green protesters
where poetry is made important by its absence
the absence of birds in a summer landscape
the lack of love in a bed at midnight
or lack of light at high noon in high places
For even bad poetry has relevance
for what it does not say
for what it leaves out
Yes what of the sun streaming down
in the meshes of morning
what of white nights and mouths of desire
lips saying Lulu Lulu over and over
and all things born with wings that sing
and far far cries upon a beach at nightfall
and light that ever was on land and sea
and caverns measured out by man
where once the sacred rivers ran
near cities by the sea
through which we walk and wander absently
astounded constantly
by the mad spectacle of existence
and all these talking animals on wheels

heroes and heroines with a thousand eyes
with bent hearts and hidden oversouls
with no more myths to call their own
constantly astounded as I am still
by these bare-faced bipeds in clothes
these stand-up tragedians
pale idols in the night streets
trance-dancers in the dust of the Last Waltz
in this time of gridlock Autogeddon
where the voice of the poet still sounds distantly
the voice of the Fourth Person Singular
the voice within the voice of the turtle
the face behind the face of the race
a book of light at night
the very voice of life as Whitman heard it
a wild soft laughter
(ah but to free it still
from the word-processor of the mind!)
And I am a reporter for a newspaper
on another planet
come to file a down-to-earth story
of the What When Where How and Why
of this astounding life down here
and of the strange clowns in control of it
the curious clowns in control of it
with hands upon the windowsills
of dread demonic mills
casting their own dark shadows
into the earth's great shadow
in the end of time unseen
in the supreme hashish of our dream

Ferlinghetti at Laugharne

Tony Curtis spoke to Lawrence Ferlinghetti on his visit to Laugharne in Wales, 14th May 1991.

Tony Curtis: Lawrence, you were last in Wales briefly in 1989 when you were on tour promoting your novel *Love in the Days of Rage*. But you had a connection with Wales many years before that, didn't you? Weren't you close to us during the war?

Lawrence Ferlinghetti: Well, I was in Plymouth harbour the night before the first day of the Normandy invasion, D-Day, and I was in Milford Haven one night, the night before that, I believe. And we were here in Cardiff the week before. I was in a small anti-submarine vessel and so on D-Day itself we left Plymouth at two in the morning, I guess, and what was memorable was coming up to Normandy and the beaches — the ships were steaming from all ports, as you know, and as the first light came up in the English Channel you could see the tops of the masts of ships in at least a hundred and eighty degree arc, all around you, behind you, just the masts of the ships silhouetted against the horizon getting light. And as the light grew, the masts became higher and more visible and came in around you like the whole horizon was this forest of masts advancing and converging on this one point off the Normandy beach-head. It was a sight I'll never forget, it was ...

TC: Rather like Birnam Wood coming to Dunsinane?

LF: Well, yes, and another parallel from Shakespeare was that the night before in all the lanes and alleys, behind all the hedgerows leading down to all the little ports the transport was packed, just lorries and lorries and American trucks and all kind of armoured vehicles jammed full of soldiers, jammed full of men sitting. I remember after it got dark you could see these fires where there were encampments, camp fires, and no noise and the fires were hooded and you weren't supposed to show any light. And you had this feeling that the whole landscape was sown with troops waiting in the darkness. And I remember it was like before the battle of Agincourt. You felt that their officers were like the King himself stalking about from campfire to campfire. And it could very well have been. Well, those are the two main memories of that time. Except there were other pleasant memories after we got back to England. We were shipwrecked in the enormous storm that came up in the week after the Normandy invasion and we had to put in

to Cowes. We were in a shipyard in Cowes and I got to go up to
London and enjoy myself in the middle of the war for a couple of
weeks. That part was, oh what a lovely war. Even though there were
buzz-bombs falling in London.

TC: Do you know the poet Alun Lewis from the Second World
War? From the British perspective the two major poets of the War
are Keith Douglas, who died in the desert in North Africa, and also
this Welshman Alun Lewis who died in Burma. He has a poem
called 'All Day it has Rained' which is something along those lines
in that it's that awful feeling of being in a bivouac tent on manoeuvres
and not actually getting to grips with the fighting. That awful lull
which is worse than the fighting itself in a way.

LF: I know that there was a lot of raining at that stage. For one thing
the invasion was scheduled to start on one day. The troops started
to get onto the ships stood out of the various harbours, and then
Eisenhower called back the whole operation on account of the
threatening weather.

TC: Have you written about all those experiences?

LF: No, I haven't. I mean to get back to it someday. Well it's a thing
to do in prose and I ... well, I hope to do it.

TC: We were at Laugharne today, which is a place you were looking
forward to going to. But while we were there, there was the distant
sound of jet planes and cannon fire. It seems that you can't escape
from that anywhere.

LF: Well, that's different today from 1944. I don't know whose
those planes were buzzing us today. But I have a feeling it's the
American Empire — the frontiers of the American Empire. We were
in Iraq just recently.

TC: So you were against that war?

LF: Oh, it was insane. There was absolutely no reason for that war.
Bush painted himself into this corner so that there was no way out.
He wanted war, he ignored all the proposals and overtures for peace
that were made. They were barely reported in the American press.
And he is also responsible for the million Kurds who were rendered
homeless. He is directly responsible in his encouragement of their
uprising. As far as I'm concerned he did it. Practically single-handedly.
Even General Schwarzkopf is rumoured to have been against it, and
wanted to do it with sanctions. The sanctions worked in Nicaragua,
but no one pointed that out. The economic sanctions worked
perfectly well down there.

TC: But, from Britain at least, it seemed the anti-Gulf War protests
were short and ineffective.

LF: Well, that's what we got in reports over here. I just came back from Spain and there they had the impression that there had been no anti-war movements in the States, and that the large majority of the population agreed with Bush's war policy. It simply wasn't so. In San Francisco alone, and in Washington, D.C. and in New York City and in Chicago there were enormous anti-war demonstrations. In San Francisco there were demonstrations of 200,000 people. Two or three of them in the course of a week. Hardly reported at all in the press. Some in the local newspapers, but not on the national television. And what you have is the mainstream media completely controlled by the government. Not the way it's done in a totalitarian country, where you have absolute repressive restrictions between law and force, but by a hand-in-glove co-operation between the government and the large corporations who own national tv networks. For instance, General Electric owns national armaments plants, including nuclear armaments plants in Pennsylvania. These huge corporations own many other types of businesses apart from television, so there is a clear conflict of interest. So you're not going to have national television news reported objectively when you have an arms manufacturer who is selling arms to the Middle East owning the stations. When you have that close co-operation between corporations and governments — in Mussolini's Italy that was known as Fascism. We have a brand of corporate Fascism going on now. I'm just giving the line, the theories of Noam Chomsky, especially his book *Manufacturing Consent*. The only way for this to be stopped is for laws to be passed saying that broadcasting companies cannot own types of businesses. But they'll never pass laws like that, because in the U.S.A. both parties are agents of corporate capitalism.

TC: In your opinion does this also apply to American publishing?

LF: Oh, no. But the trouble is that the television audience is, say, twenty times the number of people reading a daily newspaper.

TC: So, if the newspapers aren't having a big effect, what effect can poetry have?

LF:The poets remain as the only people who have the possibility of remaining not compromised. The poets are the only ones free to speak the truth, in a way. And yet so many of them give away that birthright by taking grants from the National Endowment. Or whatever they call it over here.

TC: The Arts Council. You don't agree with that?

LF: Well, it depends on whether you have a benevolent government which doesn't commit crimes against humanity. You see, in the United States you have a government which may be beneficent in giving out grants to artists and writers, but with its other hand it's killing millions of people in illegal wars overseas.

TC: But it's difficult to find a government that didn't.

LF: Well, that's the anarchist position.

TC: But if you take the Guggenheim, the National Endowment or whatever, you are then able to bite the hand that's fed you. That's justified, isn't it?

LF: I'm going from the point of view of Albert Camus who said that you're guilty of complicity if you go along with the system that operates like this. So many supposedly dissident writers and artists in the United States take the government money.

TC: W.H. Auden said that poetry made nothing happen. When the Beats in the 50s and through the 1960s had those enormous performance audiences, wasn't there a sense there that poetry could make something happen?

LF: Well, it did make a lot happen. For instance, when the Congressional Un-American Activities Committee came to San Francisco they had such a hard time they never came back. It was about the last appearance of that committee in the late 1950s or early 1960s in San Francisco. But remember that Plato banned the poets from his Republic as being too dangerous. The poet is, by definition, someone who is challenging the status quo, challenging the common accepted view of reality. That's the real function of the artist. By this definition the poet is an enemy of the state, and has to be if he's worth his salt.

TC: We've been on a pilgrimage to Laugharne today and Dylan Thomas is about the most apolitical poet you could think of. He writes about childhood; he writes about rural Wales; he writes often in a Biblical language about things.

LF: His poetry will last longer than the political poets. I mean as soon as we write a political poem we condemn ourselves to a short life. For instance, I wrote a tirade, a book about Nixon called *Tyrannus Nix*, and who wants to read that now? Who wants to read about the werewolf himself today? I mean that werewolf face of Nixon was enough to scare anyone. But no one wants to hear about that today — "Go away, don't give me that stuff". But Thomas is above all that stuff; he could get away with being above all that, you might say. A minor poet who ignored the world situation would be nowhere; there wouldn't be any reason to listen to him poetically. But it happened that Thomas was a genius with language and I don't understand what seems to be the current attitude to Dylan Thomas in both the United States and Britain, and Wales even. People put him down for having been too Romantic, too plush, too posh, too fulsome. And I don't understand that at all. This is one of the great voices of the century; poetically, probably the greatest to write in English.

TC: And you heard him in '53 at the end?

LF: Yes, I heard him twice in San Francisco, both times he was quite lushed up. His voice was very plush and very posh and his second reading was mostly devoted to poems about death by other British poets — everyone from Beddoes to Clough. And he was obsessed with death — I think he knew he was going to die. Couldn't stop drinking. And that was his last reading in the States. But I heard all the great poems in the first reading — 'Fern Hill' and 'On His Thirtieth Birthday'. I was just young then — well, I was young as a poet. About thirty. I reviewed his readings for the San Francisco art magazine at the time. And I reviewed it for the *San Francisco Chronicle* — and I said, "There is nothing like Dylan Thomas in poetry today". I still stand by that. So I don't understand why people are not imitating him still. But for one thing they can't imitate him because they don't have his talent. It was more than talent, it was genius. It was something you can't teach or learn yourself if you haven't got it, I feel. It's an intangible something that comes over the poet when he's writing, it just poured out in his case. From the stories I've heard about Thomas being a bad boy personally, it reminds me very much of the American poet Gregory Corso, who is also a bad boy, and doesn't treat his friends so well sometimes, or his women. But Corso too is an original American genius, he's an American primitive. He's never derivative of anybody. He's always completely original. I don't know whether he ever read in Wales, but he was in the famous Albert Hall reading in 1967 with Allen Ginsberg and myself and other British poets including Adrian Mitchell and Michael Horovitz.

TC: But the great art can't, in the immediate sense anyway, excuse the bad behaviour, can it? When people are hurt? Are they casualties of literature, the bystanders?

LF: Well, the bad boys pay for it. I mean it's the classic Romantic profile of the *poète maudit* who dies early. Dylan, like so many others of the genre, dying at 39.

TC: Did America kill him?

LF: Well, that's what Kenneth Rexroth said in a great poem called 'Thou shalt not kill: an elegy on the death of Dylan Thomas'. He condemns the consumer society in general, and in particular the man in the Brook Brothers suit, or the ugly American, for having killed Thomas. Of course, he drank himself to death, so he killed himself really. There's nothing like Rexroth's poem for a really vituperative castigation of American culture in particular which is now sweeping the world. It should be much better known.

TC: Perhaps Dylan's reputation has taken a downturn because we find the rhetoric too embarrassing. We want to be more streetwise. It's the Biblical echoes, the Shakepearean echoes, the big language, which, perhaps, we can't handle. Perhaps we are, both of our countries, a small screen nation now.

LF: He's too rhetorical for the postmodern period. He's like the last of the classical poets.

TC: In the 30s when he first appeared they tried to pigeon-hole him, as critics do, as a surrealist for a while. It hardly fits. Perhaps that was their way of saying — "We don't know what the hell he's doing".

LF: No, I think he was much greater than them. You have to be quite specific in saying the French Surrealists. There were American and British followers — at City Lights we republished David Gascoyne's book on Surrealism. But the surrealists I never thought were great poets *per se*. I never thought Andre Breton himself was a great poet. But Apollinaire and Cendrars were the greatest of twentieth century French poets as far as I was concerned.

TC: Coming out of a Dylan Thomas reading you were obviously affected by the sense of occasion as well as the quality of the language. Did that make you want to be up there to perform your writing?

LF: Oh, definitely. Dylan Thomas had a very definite effect on the San Francisco Renaissance which began in the early 1950s when the Beat poets arrived from New York — I'm talking about Allen Ginsberg, Gregory Corso, William Burroughs, Jack Kerouac, and others that my little publishing house ended up publishing. When they arrived in San Francisco they were all kind of New York carpet-baggers, including myself, and they were very much turned on to what's called "performance poetry" today. Up till that period poetry had been dead on the printed page. It was a very dead poetry scene with old poetry magazines like *Poetry* (Chicago) publishing these precious little anthologies — poetry about language, poetry about poetry — like it is today. It was really a dead period or a gestative period; so in the 1950s, after the war, the population flowed towards the West as though the continent had tilted, there was a *deracination*, an uprooting of everyone by the Second World War. Half the guys who went off to the war never stayed back home anymore. *How you gonna keep the boys on the farm after they've seen*

Paris? But it took up until the 1950s for this fantastic deracination to coalesce into the new configuration of literary elements. Naturally, it happened in San Francisco, which is sort of the last frontier. And the idea of most of the Beat poets was oral messages, poems that had to make it aloud first; the printed page came later, that would be incidental. It had to make it without explanation. I've always felt that the poem that had to be explained was a failure, to the extent it had to be explained. We were used to hearing the poets in the universities before that giving a five or ten minute explanation for a two minute poem. There's plenty of that right now. Our idea was to kick the sides out of all of that. If you heard Allen Ginsberg read *Howl* you'd slap yourself on the head and say, "I never saw the world like that before". That's what a great poet has to do, but how often does it happen — same with Dylan Thomas — you'd say, "I never saw reality or heard reality like that before", like it's a great new vision. So the oral bardic tradition which Thomas carried forward when he read was fantastic for many of the local San Francisco poets there.

TC: So who was there? Can you name names?

LF: Well, all kinds of poets were in San Francisco at the time — I'm not sure who went to the Dylan Thomas readings. And then the Caedmon recordings of Thomas were wonderful; it was a miracle that they survived.

TC: But I would have thought that the major influence on a lot of American poets of the 1950s was Whitman. Though, of course, not for the oral presentation of readings.

LF: Well, Allen Ginsberg claimed Walt Whitman for his homosexual side, but generally for his universal side. Allen had the same compassion that Whitman had.

TC: It's the principle of 'Song of Myself' — morally you start here, you sort yourself out and then move outwards.

LF: No, with Allen it wasn't really the song of yourself — as a Buddhist you have to suppress yourself; you can't really go around singing songs of yourself. But you can say that he sang a song of humanity. And he sang William Blake. When Allen sang *The Songs of Innocence and Experience* it was really beautiful to hear. These are songs of humanity. I think Allen Ginsberg is still the greatest living American poet. No doubt about it — a great world view. He paid homage to Dylan Thomas; he came to Wales and he wrote a long poem of his own at Fern Hill — he happened to write it on LSD, but it's a wonderful long poem in homage to Dylan Thomas. One master recognises another. And all the minor poets don't recognise

this — can't hear the eternal voice in there. You know, Allen read
that on the William Buckley show on tv and Allen is such a powerful
reader that Buckley could not interrupt him.

TC: I think the problem in Wales is that Thomas is the only writer
of ours who has had world recognition and, in a sense, he doesn't
recognise Wales. You come away with a very limited sense of what
this country really is.

LF: You mean James Joyce wasn't Welsh? [laughs]. "Well you know
it, and don't you ken it, and that's the he and the she of it."

TC: Well, perhaps we are being too chauvinistic. We ought to be
grateful for Dylan Thomas. He is a world poet — he starts with a
small canvas and it becomes enormous and important.

LF: Of course, he wasn't political in any way. Some people claimed
that he was religious. I don't see that at all. I think he was basically
a pagan poet.

TC: But you can certainly hear the preacher when he's performing
and you can locate the Bible — "the ear of the synagogue of corn"
and so on.

LF: But that was just because he grew up with those images in his
head from being around church services and Welsh preachers.

TC: Is Allen Ginsberg a religious poet?

LF: Allen is Jewish for one thing and yet his poetry is not Jewish.
Even though he wrote a long book-length poem to his mother,
Kaddish. Allen has never been classed as being a religious poet, his
poetry is not predominantly characterised as being Jewish, it seems
to me.

TC: But that's what I mean. There's the sense that the term
"religious" is used with regard to a poet such as Dylan Thomas
because he celebrates life.

LF: Ginsberg was closer to being a religious poet for his Buddhism.
I don't know about Allen Ginsberg celebrating life: I think sometimes Allen celebrates death. His poetry since the death of his
mother, since the big book *Kaddish,* has increasingly celebrated
death. He has a song he sings called 'Father Death', he does it with
his Indian music-box, like an accordion. It's like a Blake song —
"Father death be kind to me". And he has many poems that are
really obsessed with death. He's been celebrating death for a long
time now.

TC: One of the things that I respond to strongly in Dylan Thomas
is the refusal to mourn or accept, you know, "Rage, rage against the
dying of the light". Is there something about clenching the fist in a
cold northern European way about that? Like some crude Viking

warrior, some macho hero saying, "Fuck you, Death — I'm not going to take it".

LF: He's not accepting it at all. He's not celebrating it and he's not using some religious escape. He's not saying, "And death shall have no dominion because Christ the Lord is going to save me". You never hear that from Dylan Thomas.

TC: No, but there's some sense of a resurrection, though perhaps only as the flowers come up. Perhaps it's that kind of idea.

LF: I don't think you get any feeling of resurrection in Dylan Thomas's poems. I haven't.

TC: I was telling you that Vernon Watkins taught me for a while in Swansea University and Vernon, as a Christian, wanted to argue that Dylan was a Christian. I find that hard to accept, though I find that he is religious in the broader sense. But you could say that about almost any poet, couldn't you? Your own poem — "Christ climbed down / from his bare tree this year / and ran away to ...".

LF: Well, that's a satire on what modern society has done to the conception of Christ, but I also have a satire on the Lord's Prayer.

TC: And there's that hip crucifixion in *A Coney Island of the Mind* isn't there?

LF: Yes, I stole that from Lord Buckley, who was a hip white man. The first white man I ever heard talk black hip talk. He was a man who called his wife "Lady Buckley" and he called you "His Highness" and he was a kind of circus performer, charlatan in the way he dressed with robes and he swept them around him. His everyday dress was a robe or perhaps a crown or a turban. At City Lights we published a book of his jazz monologues. It was called *The Hiporama of the Classics*. He did hip versions of 'Friends, Romans, countrymen', and things like the Declaration of Independence in jive-talk And he did one called *The Naz* which was about Jesus Christ and I ripped it off for my poem on Christ.

TC: That poem is still used in school assemblies, I can testify to that. I must confess that I pinched 'Christ came down' earlier this year because my writing students were very concerned about the Gulf War and I showed them your poem and suggested that they could use your first five lines as a starting point for a structure into which they could fit specific Gulf War images. It seemed to work very well, as a kind of hook. It has a strong choric force. Is that satisfying for you? I mean, this is a poem that dates from *A Coney Island of the Mind* in 1958.

LF: Oh yes, that book is still in print — about a million copies sold. They have a public surface that anyone can understand. And then they are supposed to make it aloud, without explanations. Of course, poetry has to have several other levels — a subversive level and a subjective level — otherwise it's just journalism.

TC: Oddly, it seems to me that the quality of Dylan Thomas is that, although he sounds like a preacher, he's got this BBC veneer over his natural, though middle-class, Welsh accent. Although he sounds like a voice of authority he is, of course, radical in what he is saying. Some of the images are quite startling in the way in which they deconstruct conventional religion and conventional belief.

LF: I can see how people would start to use the word "surrealist" in talking about him because "surrealist" has been misused as meaning any kind of disparate conjunction of imagery. I mean "Garlic and sapphires in the mud / Clot the bedded axle-tree" in the *Four Quartets* — is that surrealist? I always thought that was Eliot's best poetry, not *The Waste Land*.

TC: The great American poet who didn't want to be American.

LF: Oh yes, when City Lights published Allen Ginsberg's *Howl* I wrote the jacket blurb and the first thing I said was that this was the greatest long poem to be published since Eliot's *Four Quartets* in 1943. There was a now famous reading in San Francisco in what was called the Six Gallery; it was a gallery in a garage, with maybe a hundred people at the most, half of whom were poets maybe. And Ginsberg read *Howl* for the first time there and I sent him a telegram that night using the words that Emerson used in writing to Whitman when he first received a copy of *Leaves of Grass*. He wrote to Whitman: "I greet you at the beginning of a great career." And that's what I sent to Allen. I added, "PS — when do we get the manuscript?"

TC: That sold hundreds of thousands of copies didn't it?

LF: Yes, courtesy of the San Francisco Police Department and the U.S. Customs which busted the book. And my partner and myself were put on trial and we were defended by the American Civil Rights Union — thank God for them otherwise we'd have gone out of business. And we had a criminal lawyer called Jake Ehrlich who latched onto the case when he thought he was going to get his picture in *Life Magazine*, which he did. It's hard to get that kind of publicity, especially these days. I mean, if you took your clothes off at a poetry reading today, do you think anyone would notice?

TC: So *Howl* sells because it's supposed to be outrageous, Dylan Thomas attracts attention because he's supposed to be a drunk and a womaniser — is that what you have to do to get poetry noticed, for goodness sake? It's depressing.

LF: Well, given the universal brainwash by television these days, I don't think we could do very much about that. You just have to realise that television is this electronic gadget that has somehow managed to capture the consciousness of two-thirds of the people on earth. You don't have to be slaves to this thing. Poetry — with all the media that you have these days, the single unaccompanied voice doesn't have much of a chance. If I were a young, twenty or twenty-five-year-old poet I would go into film and video. In fact, I think that's where all the young poets are going in the States. The ones who would have become poets are all doing video. They're video-poets.

TC: So is poetry weak at the moment in the States?

LF: It's very academic. There's a lot of language about language, poetry about poetry. But some new young turk will come along and make a great new barbaric yawp.

TC: But what about some of the old turks doing that, Lawrence? What about that? You obviously felt strongly about the Gulf War — did you write about that?

LF: Well, no. It seems like older poets are baffled into silence [laughs]. It seems like it's impossible to utter some great, all-encompassing statement these days. But even as I say that I realise that one of these days some turk is going to come along and give out a new, barbaric yawp (that was Whitman's term) and knock the sides out of everything again. And everyone will stand around saying, "Gee, why didn't I think of that — it was so obvious — it was just waiting to be said".

Poet as Fisherman

As I grow older I perceive
Life has its tail in its mouth
and other poets other painters
are no longer any kind of competition
It's the sky that's the challenge
the sky that still needs deciphering
even as astronomers strain to hear it
with their huge electric ears
the sky that whispers to us constantly
the final secrets of the universe
the sky that breathes in and out
as if it were the inside of a mouth
of the cosmos
the sky that is the land's edge also
and the sea's edge also
the sky with its many voices and no god
the sky that engulfs a sea of sound
and echoes it back to us
as in a wave against a seawall
Whole poems whole dictionaries
rolled up in a thunderclap
And every sunset an action painting
and every cloud a book of shadows
through which wildly fly
the vowels of birds about to cry
And the sky is clear to the fisherman
even if overcast
He sees it for what it is:
a mirror of the sea
about to fall on him
in his wood boat on the dark horizon
We have to think of him as the poet
forever face to face with old reality
where no birds fly before a storm
And he knows what's coming down
before the dawn

and he's his own best lookout
listening for the sound of the universe
and singing out his sightings
of the land of the living

Helen Dunmore
An Unlikely Ambition

It's that moment of silence just after a poetry reading when the questions are due to begin. Just before the smiles become fixed and the organiser glances round and then leans forward with her prepared question, someone raises a hand:

"Have you always wanted to be a poet? — and how long have you been writing poetry?"

This must be one of the questions most commonly asked of poets, both in public forums and private conversations. The more I am asked it, the harder I find it to answer. We may live in a society which is shy of the word "vocation", but even so the decision to become a poet is not made in the same way as the decision to become an electrical engineer. The two careers do have one thing in common, however, in that a little girl born in the early nineteen-fifties was about as unlikely to be encouraged towards the one as the other. So why didn't I discard the ambition to become a poet as soon as it formed? It seems to me now that the first, necessary "work" of a poet is to believe that he or she can become one. I suspect that for many poets this belief isn't achieved once and for all at one particular point, but comes in stages.

My first, naïve faith in myself as a poet crystallised early on, at seven or eight. At that time, fortunately, it did not need external validation. There was no question of "becoming" a poet at some later date when my poems were published, because my most important sense of self was already knitted up with a response to poetry and a longing to echo that response through writing my own poems.

My models were male. They had to be. The one woman poet I had heard of was Christina Rossetti, and then I only knew her *Goblin Market*. I noticed women's names in hymn-books, and loved the anonymous voices of ballad and nursery rhyme, which some feminist commentators now take to be the hidden voices of women composing for the voice rather than for paper. But I don't think it occurred to me then that all the poetry books I read were written by men, or that there might be something in maleness which fitted or entitled an individual to write poetry. I surfed through bookshelves until I found something I could use, absorbing it and mimicking it until I'd made it my own, then catching the next wave. In the houses of my childhood (we moved often) books lay about in heaps, fell off shelves or were stacked on the floor. A child could mine through them and believe that no one else had ever opened these dark, shining seams. A poem which captured my imagination was not necessarily one I understood. It became mine even though I didn't quite know what to do with it. At primary school in the late fifties and early sixties we caught the tail end of the tradition that poetry should be learned by heart, and the poems which I learned then I possessed with a peculiar sensuous immediacy. Like spells, they could be called up at will to the ear and to the tongue. I repeated lines jealously in my head, in the way I would later work from a small, echoing phrase to a whole poem.

At eight or so I was given a stack of thin card which came directly from a paper factory. I had been taken round the factory and knew how the porridgy soup of pulp became my pile of smooth pale green sheets. I worked my way down the pile of unused card as if I was excavating an unknown geology: a geology which could not exist until I had marked it out with my pencil as I lay on my stomach in front of the fire. I rhymed relentlessly, and drilled my poems into metre until they were as durable as wooden boxes. My sonnets might wear strait-jackets, but they were sonnets and that was the point of them. At this time the content of my poems was remorselessly subdued to the demands of form. I think that the poems on which I worked with such passionate enjoyment must have been very banal, but that scarcely mattered to me. While I was writing them I loved them, and then I let them disappear in the way children allow their drawings and writings to vanish. At that time the process of drafting took place not just within each poem, but from poem to poem, so that whole swathes of writing existed only in order to be discarded. Each poem was a stepping-stone without which I would not have built in sufficient technique to advance, but nobody digs up stepping-stones and carry them on the rest of the journey.

This interest in the process has remained with me, and so has the belief that whole poems are written not as ends in themselves, but in order to take the writer to the point where she can write other poems. It can be very hard to acknowledge that a poem which has walked about in one's imagination for weeks, and taken hours of work, is not actually of any significance in itself and ought to be torn up. Good thinking can most certainly lead to bad poems. But then, a little while later, I find myself realising that the next poem is built on the territory explored by the destroyed poem. For this reason I like to clear out folders and get rid of poems from time to time, rather than keep everything which contains a promising phrase or two. I've always found it exhilarating once those clotted, worked-over pages are in the bin.

Another part of the process of writing poems which I have come to appreciate more and more is the first stage of writing a way into a poem, making marks which can be as crude as they need to be in order to define the territory of the poem. This primitive map-making is often shot through with one or two fully-formed phrases which embody the essential music of the poem, the sound which the ear follows and seeks to shape. So these early drafts may offer a startling contrast between writing which is done for the sake of getting somewhere else, and perfect fragments of the poem as it will become. As a collection of poems develops, something similar happens on a larger scale. At a certain point I realise not just that these poems are beginning to form a collection, but what kind of collection it is going to be. The poems talk to one another. There's an exchange of ideas, and an intricate web of language: touched at one point, it vibrates at another. I become more and more interested in the shaping of the collection, and again there's the question of discarding work. A good poem may sit uneasily in a particular book, just as an image can be beautiful but fail to function in a poem.

For several years now I have used a word-processor to work on my poems. I write novels as well as poetry, and I've noticed that people find it more acceptable to think of novels being written on-screen than poems. Perhaps it offends the idea that poetry-writing is a highly mysterious, even mystical activity, not to be contaminated by technology. A poet should write on napkins in cafes, or crouch at his desk in his room under the eaves, sailing a rough sea of paper, writing furiously with the pen he's used all his life while down below his wife smilingly silences the children ... Ah yes, the wife, the children, the blessed absolution from daily life, and the pen moving across the paper. I'll return to them soon.

On the other hand there is the word-processor. If you touch-type, as I do, it provides the closest thing I can imagine to the sensation of being inside one's own brain. Words rise, glowing, to form patterns which dissolve or re-form at will. Lines and stanzas move around, trying out their places. Tiny stored phrases find their sockets. The poem fails and disappears, to begin again beside the small pulse of the cursor. The whole thing remains infinitely fluid; even printing is no longer a definitive act but something which can be done a hundred times, once for each new variation. The word-processor has moved beyond the mechanical into something as meltingly lateral as thought itself. And besides, it frees me from the awkward handwriting of a left-hander obliged at school to learn a style which is only suitable for right-handers. I do use a notebook, but only because I can't take the word-processor everywhere. I dream of a small, perfect laptop the size of a Woolworth's exercise book, with batteries as durable as diamonds.

The word-processor seems to harmonise perfectly with another stage in the process by which I write poems: this is composition in the head, often when out walking, or late at night before sleeping. Sometimes this is only a question of working over a few lines, particularly where there's a problem to solve, but at other times line after line rises, fed by the rhythm of a long walk or the semi-drowse of the mind disengaging, ready for sleep. I've learned that it's essential to memorise these lines thoroughly, for they can disappear as readily as they came, like the perfect idea for a short story which burst on Thomas Hardy as he was working in his cold frame. Sure that he would remember something so good, he continued to garden. By the time he went back to the house the idea had gone without trace, leaving only an itch in his mind which he was never able to scratch. Composing in my head has become vital to me for two reasons, one artistic and one practical. The first is that the poem grows against the ear, and can be heard from its earliest stages. It is easy to sense the build-up of a sound structure, and to work out how to develop this. The second, more practical reason for this "writing in the head" is that I am not able to write whenever I want: that is, it may be possible to jot down a few words at any time, but not to begin the intense work of forming a poem on paper or the screen.

This brings me to the second question most commonly asked at poetry readings: "Do you write at regular times, or do you wait for inspiration?". It also connects to the image of the poet writing in his secluded, protected space, serviced by his muse/wife. Like many other poets, I find that this image has little to do with my own life. As I grew up my first, naïve assumption that I was a poet and would write poems had to confront some alarming economic and social facts. I would have to earn a living, and if I wanted to have children I would not have a wife to look after them. If I did not watch out I would be that "wife" myself, or worse still the "old lady" of someone who valued his creativity far above mine. No one who does not remember the late sixties and early seventies can imagine how dauntingly chauvinistic the musicians and poets of that time could be. When I was twenty I moved to Finland and lived there for two years, knowing many poets and musicians but never mentioning that I myself wrote poetry, because I wished to protect it from the belittlement I saw handed out to other young women with similar ambitions. A year or so later, when I began to publish my poems, I "came out" as a poet for a second time, not with quite the spontaneity of my childhood but with a much deeper understanding of what it was going to mean to me to be a woman poet in my society. It meant, above all, that there were very few patterns to follow. Things have changed enormously for women poets in the past twenty years, and for a young woman beginning her work now there are many very different models of how she might proceed. It's possible to hear the title of the Bloodaxe anthology *Sixty Women Poets* as a cry of triumph. That book would have been unimaginable when I was twenty-one.

But although there were huge problems about defining oneself as a woman poet in the England of the early seventies, there was also a great sense of excitement. Nobody knew what achievements might be possible. I believed that there were ways of writing poems which had not as yet even been imagined, and subject matter which had not made its way into those rows of published poetry books. When I was writing the poems for my first collections my main working time was the mornings when my baby usually slept. If he did not I had the playpen beside me and would drop in a different toy as I shot back the carriage return. The trick was not to see this as an inferior method of working, compared to an ideal of endless available time and the servicing of one's creativity by others. It was to see it as an exploration.

I walked and walked, pushing my pram, composing in my head, ready for the next burst of available time. I began to see that there were real advantages in this method, not least in that the concept of writer's block simply disappeared, just as the concept of insomnia disappears when you are never allowed enough sleep. I was always having to leave poems as they came tantalisingly to life, and so I was always hungry to return to them. I still find that I work best when I leave a piece of writing while it is going well, rather than when I reached a difficult stage and so will find myself reluctant to return to it. However, I do agree with the American writer Tillie Olsen when she says that there are few lives more exhausting than that of the woman writer and mother who also has a paid job to support her writing or her household. Often over the past fifteen or so years I've had the sense of every faculty being stretched beyond what I'd thought possible; but again, this isn't always disagreeable. It has made me realise how much can be done in a given, relatively short space of time, and how a writer can learn to see other activities as

part of writing rather than as distractions from it. It would be sad
to wish one's life away, always longing to be elsewhere and writing
about it. On the other hand the thought of Mrs Gaskell writing in
the centre of her house with all the doors open so that she had her
finger perpetually on the pulse of the household does make me
shiver.

One thing my experience has given me is a very strong commitment
to support and encourage other writers, and a sense that one's work
as a poet is not only an individual vocation, but also part of a wider
work. Poets, perhaps more than prose writers, tend to know one
another, to form relationships on reading tours and during residen-
cies, to share long journeys, horrific hotel rooms and poor pay. We
send each other poems in draft, we review one another's work. It's
incestuous, perhaps, but it seems a necessary closeness. Certain
friendships have been crucial to my work, giving confidence and
encouraging me to push beyond the boundaries of what I could
already do. We do live in a very individualistic society, where talent
is seen as a marketable commodity and competition is encouraged
by a system of prizes and "Best of British Poets" or "Best of British
Novelists" promotions. If these aim to raise the profile of poetry or
the novel, fine, but it is sad if they come to pit writer against writer
in an uneasy consciousness that the brief searchlight of publicity
only picks out a few names. It is sadder still if competition causes
poets to shrink away from an appreciative understanding of each
other's talents, and to collude in a media-orientated pecking-order.
We have a common work which belongs to none of us. I come back
to the anonymous voices of song and ballad, where the names of the
writers have peeled away in the racing stream of time.

Drafting of 'In the Desert Knowing Nothing'

These drafts illustrate the development of a poem which was written as an immediate response to an event: the Gulf War, 1991. The first, handwritten drafts were written in my kitchen on the night of 24 January 1991. At this stage no one was yet sure what the scale of destruction in the Gulf might be. I had been in bed, but the poem began to form so insistently in my mind that I came downstairs, found the notebook, began to write. It was long after midnight, and raining.

It's not uncommon for poems to begin late at night in this way, and I've learned that I need to get up and write down the lines immediately because they will be lost if I wait until morning. I can tell from the handwriting on this draft that the poem was written very fast, with words discarded as soon as they were written down. My habit of working from right to left page is also shown: I often do this in notebooks and I think it is because I'm left-handed.

The skeleton of the poem comes out strongly from the first draft. There are one or two lines which will be dropped, and the order will change. The three lines scribbled into a verse on the first handwritten sheet will be developed into three separate verses. The sound pattern of the poem (which depends on the manipulation of repetitions) will form later that night as the poem is transferred to the word-processor. Within a day the poem is finished, though I remember spending a lot of time on its layout: these differently laid-out drafts were not kept. A short time later I received a request for a poem from Stephen Parr, who was preparing a poem broadsheet on the Gulf War. I sent him 'In the Desert Knowing Nothing'. This broadsheet, called *Writers on the Storm*, was published during the Gulf War, and distributed throughout Avon. Public readings were given from it by the poets involved. The poem was next printed in *Poetry Review*'s special issue on the Gulf War, *A Hundred Harms* (Summer 1992), and later collected in in *Recovering a Body* (Bloodaxe, 1994).

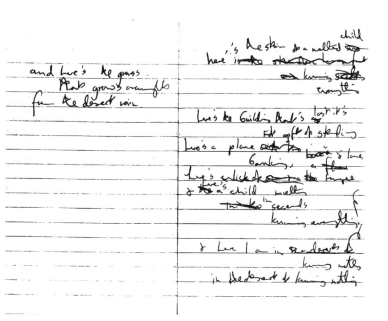

29/1/91

Here is I am in the desert,
knowing nothing

Here I am knowing nothing
in the desert & knowing
nothing

Here I am in the wild wild wide
desert long after midnight

Here is or man on the telephone,
knowing something

Here's the taut gazelle staring thru the
camera, knowing smile

Here's the boy washing his kit in a
tarpaulin, knowing
smile

and here's the grass
that grows everywhere
for the desert rain

's the skin of a melted child
here is the skeleton
or knowing something
everything

Here's the building that's lost it's
top off of sterling

Here's a plane
banking, a flame & love

Here's a click
& here's a child melting
in ten seconds
knowing everything

& Here I am in the desert &
knowing nothing
in the desert & knowing nothing

In The Desert Knowing Nothing

Here I am in the desert knowing nothing,
here I am knowing nothing
in the desert of knowing nothing,
here I am in this wide ~~ride~~ wild wide
desert long after midnight

here I am knowing nothing
hearing the noise of the rain
and the melt of fat in the pan

here is our man on the phone knowing something
in combat jeans and a clip microphone
testing for sound,
catching the desert rain, knowing something,

here's the general who's good with his men
storming the camera, knowing something
in the pit of his Americanness
here's the general taut in his battledress
and knowing something

Here's the boy washing his kit in a tarpaulin
on a front-line he knows from his GCSE
coursework on Wilfrid Owen
and knowing something

here is the plane banking,
the *go go go* of adrenalin
the child melting

and here's the grass that grows overnight
from the desert rain, feeling for him
and knowing everything

and here I am knowing nothing
in the desert of knowing nothing
dry from not speaking.

In The Desert Knowing Nothing

Here I am in the desert knowing nothing,
here I am knowing nothing
in the desert of knowing nothing,
here I am in this wide
desert long after midnight

here I am knowing nothing
hearing the noise of the rain
and the melt of fat in the pan

here is our man on the phone knowing something
and here's our man fresh from the briefing
in combat jeans and a clip microphone
testing for sound,
catching the desert rain, knowing something,

here's the general who's good with his men
storming the camera, knowing something
in the pit of his Americanness
here's the general taut in his battledress
and knowing something

Here's the boy washing his kit in a tarpaulin
on a front-line he knows from his GCSE
coursework on Wilfrid Owen
and knowing something

here is the plane banking,
the *go go go* of adrenalin
the child melting

and here's the grass that grows overnight
from the desert rain, feeling for him
and knowing everything
and here I am knowing nothing
in the desert of knowing nothing
dry from not speaking.

Final draft.

Simon Armitage

Goalkeeper With A Cigarette

That's him in the green, green cotton jersey,
prince of the clean sheets, some upright insect
boxed between the sticks, the horizontal
and the pitch, stood with something up his sleeve,
armed with a pouch of tobacco and skins
to roll his own, or else a silver tin
containing eight or nine already rolled.
That's him with one behind his ear, between
his lips, or one tucked out of sight and lit —
a stamen cupped in the bud of his fist.
That's him sat down, not like those other clowns,
performing acrobatics on the bar, or press-ups
in the box, or running on the spot,
togged out in turtleneck pyjama-suits
with hands as stunted as a bunch of thumbs,
hands that are bandaged or swaddled with gloves,
laughable, frying-pan, sausage-man gloves.
Not my man, though, that's not what my man does;
a man who stubs his reefers on the post
and kicks his heels in the stud-marks and butts,
lighting the next from the last, in one breath
making the save of the year with his legs,
taking back a deep drag on the goal-line
in the next; on the one hand throwing out
or snaffling the ball from a high corner,
flicking off loose ash with the other. Or
in the freezing cold with both teams snorting
like flogged horses, with captains and coaches
effing and jeffing at backs and forwards,
talking steam, screaming exhausting orders,
that's not breath coming from my bloke, it's smoke.
Not him either goading the terraces,
baring his arse to the visitor's-end

and dodging the sharpened ten-pence pieces,
playing up, picking a fight, but that's him
cadging a light from the ambulance men,
loosing off smoke rings, zeros or halos
that drift off, passively, over the goals
into nobodies face, up nobodies nose.
He is what he is, does whatever suits him,
because he has no highfalutin song
to sing, no neat message for the nation
on the theme of genius or dedication;
in his passport, under 'occupation',
no one forced the man to print the word
'custodian', and in *The Faber Book
of Handy Hints*, his five line entry reads:
'You young pretenders, keepers of the nought,
the nish, defenders of the sweet fuck-all,
think bigger than your pockets, profiles, health;
better by half to take a sideways view,
take a tip from me and deface yourselves.'

*Sometime during the seventies I went with a friend and his dad to Old
Trafford to see Manchester United at home to Juventus. By rights I was
a Huddersfield Town fan, so by definition I'd never seen European
football and I'd never seen fifty thousand people at a match. I'd never
seen a floodlit game either, and I was dumbstruck as we dropped on to
the terrace, hypnotised by the luminous green pitch. I felt like I was looking
out over an enormous snooker table, and the black night beyond all that
brightness confirmed the sensation.*

*A couple of minutes before kick-off the teams came rolling out of the
tunnel, and Dino Zoff, the Juventus goalkeeper, came trotting towards
the Stretford End where we were standing. Zoff's name was well known,
not just because it was a single pronounceable syllable beginning with the
last letter of the alphabet, but because he was famous. As he reached the
penalty area, he was greeted with a light smattering of applause, and to
collect the appreciation he raised his arm and held his index finger in the
air, a gesture that indicated his status as the world's number one and
therefore worthy of such a generous reception. That was his big mistake.
Suddenly he was staring at ten thousand outstretched arms, each*

supporting two fingers or a fist, and the insults and threats speared towards him as the crowd transcended all barriers between the English language and Italian. Zoff visibly faltered, and for the rest of the first half he was a nervous figure between the posts, vulnerable and exposed, just a coin's throw away.

If the incident was premeditated and designed to put Zoff off his game then it certainly worked, but on the night I remember witnessing something more spontaneous and more telling. Zoff's error was to abuse the appreciation, grudgingly shown to him, by applying it to his ego rather than his ability, and at that moment he invoked the fury of his audience by converting praise into self-importance. There was an unspoken but long-lasting feeling of satisfaction that evening experienced by a crowd whose priceless contribution had been to remind a would-be god that he was nothing better than a very good goalie.

Without the benefits of carbon dating or some type of telemetry to pin down the precise age of 'Goalkeeper With A Cigarette', I'm left with the literary equivalent of counting its teeth or taking a cross-section and totting up its rings, and I'll probably only get as far as its star sign rather than the actual date of birth or moment of conception. The first drafts are written in blue ink from a fountain pen given to me as a present in May 1993 (the receipt is still in the box), and as a general rule I make a point of avoiding that kind of writing implement. Despite being right handed, my handwriting tends to incline from the south-east to the north-west, and my middle finger trawls behind the nib, smearing and smudging anything that doesn't dry in a split second. Fibre-tips are my preferred choice, or failing that, cartographic pens, or pencils, especially the ones sharpened with a pen-knife such as those worn behind the ears of apprentice-trained carpenters or family butchers. It's been suggested to me that my cramped and cowering style of writing says much about me as a pupil, not wanting teachers or other students to see my work, but in actual fact it's the result of having the desk next to the wall, the one without any elbow room. A for Armitage — first seat on the left please. At the time of writing this, I'm using a very chubby but manageable ball-point which I won in a raffle in a pub two weeks ago. I don't ever remember winning a raffle before and for that reason saw the pen as a sign or omen and felt obliged to use it. As they presented me with the prize, someone in the pool room shouted "That'll come in handy", and they weren't wrong, as it happens.

Anyhow, May '93, although the actual idea for the poem had been brought by the stork some six or seven months earlier in the shape of a newspaper article or letter, possibly in *The Guardian*, possibly in *The Independent*. A number of football fans were recalling goal-keepers, real and imaginary, who were remembered for smoking cigarettes (and a pipe in one case) during sustained periods of attack by their own teams, and I read the newspaper on a train between London and Sherborne, in Dorset. I remember being struck immediately by its possibilities, and it wasn't really a question of whether or not I'd write about it, just a question of when and how. Getting round to it. Getting down to it. I recounted the article to a few friends, some poets, some footballers, and I watched their eyes and their smiles widen appreciably, so I felt that the idea at least was worth treating, and that hopefully I could bring something of myself to it. I probably could have got stuck into the poem there and then, but I make all this fuss about dates and places to introduce the following points: firstly, I go in fear of inspiration; it looks good in the shop, but every time I get it home it needs altering or even taking back and exchanging. Keep the receipt. Secondly, most poems are like certain cuts of meat — tempting rare, but in practice they need to be well done, done well. Third, I didn't hang on to the idea like Berryman clinging on to his Bradstreet line, like a life-raft, but I did send it to the back of the queue to let it sweat a bit. And fourth, I don't bury finished poems for years on end after completion, like Frost, then produce them in later life and reckon to have written them the previous evening. That must be damaging to creativity, but nevertheless, twelve months after applying the final full stop to 'Goalkeeper With A Cigarette' it still hadn't seen the light of day.

In the summer of '93 I was working on a series of very tightly controlled pieces, engineered and constructed things that probably owed more to mathematics than to linguistics, very gardened, very decimalized, and I couldn't simply abandon those poems or switch mode to work on the goalkeeper idea which I anticipated having a very different tone and temperament, as well as a more flexible form. I'd also been working in iambics, heartbeats, and I knew that it would be difficult getting back to a more interrupted line made up of palpitations and murmurs; going from a regular foot to a hop, skip and a jump required a change of territory as well as a change of tune, and I reckoned that the penalty area was the right place to bring about such a shift. When I first started writing poetry my normal practice was to compose in lines of ten syllables without falling into a regular rhythm. I compared each sestet, I'm afraid, with an over bowled in a cricket match, thinking that it was too predictable to serve up the same line and length each time, and that every now and again a phrase or word should sit up off the seam and go flying past the reader's ear. That same summer I'd also been figuring on writing something longer, and for that specific purpose I eventually transferred from a hardback A6 notebook to an A4 version in the same series, thinking that on a bigger pitch I might be a able to spread the play wide on the wing, or run with the ball — the full stop — as oppose to touching it down in the first available space as the closing moment of some perfectly executed set piece. Or trying to get rid of it like a hot potato. Subconsciously, I probably knew that the goalkeeper idea comprised enough material to stretch far beyond a sonnet or sestina, and that its vocabulary could provide the bridge I'd been looking for to get back to that earlier style of composition.

It's probably worth saying that I'm reluctant to begin work on a poem unless I have the title, the first line and the last, or at least a clear idea of what they should contain. I suppose I've been brought up to believe in that triumvirate as the holy trinity of a poem, around which everything else must congregate. More than that, I'm probably still playing the part of the small boy being sent on an errand by his mother, and in that situation I want to be told where to go, why, and what to say when I get there. In the case of 'Goalkeeper With A Cigarette' the title didn't take much sorting out and might well have come to me instantly, even if I did consider other candidates before rejecting them and appointing the original applicant. Looking at my notes, I see that 'Last Of The Smoking Goalkeepers' was one possibility, and 'The Goalkeeper And The Cigarette' was another, along with other variations and permutations on the same theme. Portraiture, I suppose, was at the back of my mind, and for that reason I was aiming for a title that could sit at the top of a poem or at the bottom of a painting, and be equally at home in either position. I was also thinking of those cigarette cards that carried hand-drawn images of sporting celebrities; cigarette cards rather than their modern day equivalents which involve high-gloss photography and puncture-repair-kit bubble gum. And if form should reflect content, or at least acknowledge it in some way, then at a very early stage I presumed that the poem would be one block of text in a shape befitting a portrait, a canvas on which to sketch, then draw, then colour the hero of the poem.

A further point about titles — I insist on setting them flush with the left-hand margin, and not only for visual reasons. Titles, I think, like poets, should earn respect rather than presume it. Those titles which are centrally justified seem pompous and extravagant to me, of another age, although essentially they become nothing more than nails or picture hooks from which the poem dangles. Apt, possibly, for a portrait, but titles should be working parts that can open or close a poem, or devices on which a poem can swing, and the best place for such a hinge is snug against frame. For the same reason I'm always suspicious of contemporary poets who deploy upper case letters at the beginning of every line, except at the beginning of a sentence of course. For one thing I find it visually unappealing, like a fire escape bolted on to the side of a fabulous building, and in certain poems it is indeed something of a safety precaution. And it's such a grand gesture, one that champions the notion that poetry is something given from above rather than taken from conversational language here on the ground. Having said that, some authors do have the right to assemble a ladder of capital letters down the left-hand side of a poem, either because they've earned it or because their allegiances or affiliations allow them connections and associations with other poets and other poems. Either way, I'm not one of them. In another sense it's like buying all the kit and looking good without being able to play the game. Beware of the poem with perfect teeth and day-glo lipstick — when it opens its mouth it might have nothing to say. Watch out also for capitalised nouns, lower case I's and any other form of grammatical sleight of hand that relies on trickery rather than magic and quite often fills a gap where the poet couldn't be bothered, or just couldn't. In this category I should also mention punctuation, which, metaphorically, I think of as serving a percussive function in the symphony of a poem, and should never forget its place or get under the feet of letters and their endless acoustic possibilities. I'm wary and weary of poetry reduced to a morse code of such signals; bring on the words, that's what I say.

Bring on the first line, which in this case happens to be "That's him in the green, green cotton jersey". John Ashbery once said in an interview that he aimed for two good ideas in every line, and I think that's a minimum requirement, although someone like Les Murray is a far better practitioner of that axiom than Ashbery himself, and in any case a first line should aim even higher than that. I button-hole the goalie here, single him out in the green of the pitch and the green of his jersey, which is both garment and fabric. As for the shirt itself, I associate green ones with the golden age of goalkeeping — Shilton, Clemence, Banks, Bonnetti, Stepney — thus distinguishing my man from the assortment of would-be's and wanna-be's in their technicolour dream coats that this era has offered so far. That repetition (green, green) so early in a poem struck me as unusual and worthwhile (although I could have been thinking of Auden's "As I walked out one evening, / Walking down Bristol Street") and the comma between those two words hopefully acts as a fulcrum, tipping the reader into the second half of the line and then into the rest of the poem by providing enough momentum to carriage-return to line two. The first line also announces the poem's rhythmic intentions, or lack of them in any strict metrical sense, just as the elision of the first word says something about the manner of address. I'd wondered at one stage about writing the poem as monologue or soliloquy, but because modesty and humility are two of its themes that was never a viable option. Praise from a distance was more appropriate. All of my rough drafts and original workings have that same first line, so I'm tempted to think and then say that it came to me at once and acted thereafter as a very sturdy curtain rail from which the rest of the poem could hang.

I've always told myself, and everyone else as well therefore, that I never actually sit down in front of a piece of paper when I want to write, as if I suffered from acute snow-blindness when faced with all that whiteness. Also, for a long time I deluded myself with the notion that all my composition takes place in the car, in the bath, on the hoof, off the cuff, and that by taking a couplet or envoi out for the day I can endlessly re-shuffle the word order at my leisure until sound merges with sense and rhyme matches with reason. In actual fact this is only a small part of the process, and there does come a time when the confrontation between myself and a blank sheet becomes a necessary part of the creative process — a competitive challenge, so to speak, and the lines composed away from the page beforehand are rehearsals of tactics and manoeuvres that might come in useful in bringing about victory. This is particularly true for me in the case of very formal work where shape and sequence are everything. In attempting to bring about some element of synthesis through the work as a whole, or a continuity of thought, it becomes imperative to see the poem written down. I've never actually composed on a word-processor although I do submit the final product to screen and disk, mainly for reasons of presentation, revision, reproduction and safe-keeping. I type with two fingers, the trigger finger of each hand, and through fear of ever having to type anything more than once I make pretty damn sure I've finished with a poem before I freeze it in print. My worry about actually composing on a word-processor comes from that argument about all technology when applied to creativity; I'm no Luddite, far from it, but I do think that those who master the intricacies of a Wordperfect programme and all of its wonderful facilities suddenly believe themselves to be in control of their writing, especially when it comes to line breaks or moving blocks of words from one position to another. Furthermore it doesn't lend itself to drafting or archive evidence of technique, and also deprives the author of the opportunity of flogging page upon page of hand-written scribble to American Universities for big dollars. My criterion for knowing or feeling that I have taken a poem as far as I can is to sit back, read through, and wait for that fuckin'-hell-*I*-wrote-that feeling. I haven't been writing long enough to know if that particular test is any use when it comes to gauging a poem's shelf-life or measuring its life line, although I haven't yet had that oh-fuckin'-hell-did-I-write-that feeling when looking over old poems. Well, not that I'm admitting to.

When it comes to the last line, the hem of the poem, I begin to think long and hard about what a poem means, or rather what I mean by it, and then I suppose I attempt to tie the thing up in a neat bow ready for handing over. Once again, my workings suggest that the last line in this poem was always there or thereabouts: "take a tip from me and deface yourselves", although it looks as though the word "me" was "him" at one point. I still can't decide whether the word "tip" is a felicitous play on words or a terrible pun, but anyway I'm sticking with it. "Deface" I mean literally in terms of spoiling a silhouette or profile by adding a cigarette, but I'm also advocating that trainee 'keepers risk ill-health if it comes naturally, or at least contradict professional expectations. Image, I suppose, is what I'm driving at. It's not unusual for me to try to execute some half rhyme, near rhyme, close rhyme, para rhyme (or whatever they're called this week) as part and parcel of a closing gesture, and in this scenario I'm offering "health" and "... selves", hoping that the sounds are still chiming after leap-frogging the penultimate line.

And what is the poem about? Well, I hope that it speaks for itself of course, and the Dino Zoff parable at the front of this article was by way of explanation as well as entertainment. There's been plenty of chatter of late, lots of twittering about the role and status of the poet in contemporary society, and maybe in the poem I'm putting poets in the role of custodian, suggesting that their position is at the back, the last line of defence, or I'm saying that the poet's task is to hold the line, let nothing past. Maybe I'm trying to invert the footballing cliché that attack is the best method of defence. But if the poem succeeds it should do so through sensation and feeling

rather than observation and understanding — Pound's thing about
actually experiencing an idea rather than simply comprehending it
— and it's probably for that reason that I'm happy to let the poem
stand or fall or sink or swim on its own without my attaching guy
ropes or armbands to it. I hope it achieves "that click" as Frost put
it. The strongest feeling I have about what poetry is and what poetry
does is to do with similitude and coupling, the connecting of one
idea to another through sound and sense. That's when a poem clicks
into place for me, so that's what I'm always after.

There is a way in which that brings into relief the question of why
I write poetry in the first place, and leading on from that, who I write
it for. I think the first part of that can be answered very neatly with
the joke "Why do dogs lick their bollocks? Because they can". I
prefer that explanation rather than a re-appropriation of Sir
Edmund Hilary's line "Because they're there", since the latter
pre-supposes that poems are already written and are simply waiting
to be collected by persons with the necessary qualifications. As for
audience, I believe in all that dualism business which says that every
writer is communicating with him or herself on all sorts of different
levels, and I also believe that creativity is wholeheartedly connected
with childhood, innocence and naïvety, or the loss of it, in a way
that I haven't been able to express as yet. And memory also, as if all
writers are driven by the unbearable burden of nostalgia, the irre-
trievable, whether for past life, lost life, or even for events and
thoughts that happened only two, three, four seconds ago. Allied to
this, I think, are the metaphors and analogies that poets apply to
their own creative procedure: Hughes stalking his animals, Durrell
catching a lizard without pulling its tail off, Frost clearing a lump in
his throat, Graves imagining himself somewhere in history, Eliot
drawing the curtain up and down, Valery following up the clue of
the first line, Blake being dictated to, Sexton seeing it as "a little
cause, something to do no matter how rotten I was", Lowell turning
the doorknob of a poem, Pound looking to create order rather than
split the atom, and so on. So I'm really suggesting that audience and
author are one and the same. Glenn Gould: "I have captured, I
think, an atmosphere of improvisation which I don't believe has
been captured in Brahms recordings before. There is a quality as
though — this isn't an original comment but something one of my
friends said — as though I were really playing for myself, but left
the door open". Outside of that but no less real comes the gallery
of faces peering over every poet's shoulder, and in my case that's
made up of teachers, friends, my parents, my wife, critics and

professors that I've never met and of course other poets. The two poets that I feel a responsibility and an accountability to are Hughes and Harrison, both for reasons of locality and speech, and I tend to think of them as forefathers or godfathers in terms of the poetics of this region.

There probably isn't much mileage in going on to explain or excuse the rest of the poem line by line by line — its construction extends from most of the methodologies and principles already outlined — and on that basis I estimate that the remainder of it is self-explanatory. But I will describe some of the other ideologies and techniques that I generally employ — guidelines rather than tramlines — or conventions that I stick by or depart from. As far as line breaks are concerned, I try to avoid hatcheting groups of words that fall into a natural cluster, which isn't always easy when using a syllabic framework. I'm always conscious of using form rather than letting form dictate the poem, but form can be a very slippery customer, like Dirk Bogarde in *The Servant,* and before you know it you're buttering its toast and ironing its shirts. If I can break a line on a hard noun or at the end of a sentence then I will, unless a more unorthodox break can produce extra effect without looking forced or uncomfortable or embarrassed. As for diction, I sometimes build up an inventory or stockade of words and phrases during the early stages of a poem, then take from it. I quite often end up using two words in a poem that are sister words or counterparts, twinned either by sound, shape or meaning; "swaddled" and "snaffling" is the best example I can identify in this poem. There's always a point at which I wander over to the reference section of the bookcase and pull out a thesaurus, but in most cases it only throws up a list of words I've already rejected. Books like those are full of words that anyone or everyone can use, and I suppose that poets are looking for something belonging to themselves, or something more refractory. Poetry might well be the best words in the best order, but that suggests the existence of the right word, whereas a poem quite often requires the wrong word and a thesaurus doesn't allow for that degree of latitude. For myself, my own word pool has more to do with the West Riding than with precise lexicographical categories, and if a word hasn't passed through the hands of my friends, family or heroes then it doesn't even get a look in, let alone an interview.

Many of my original drafts are totally illegible. Sometimes its because I'm writing too fast trying to catch a line before it evaporates, but mostly it's because I'm only sketching in a sentence or stanza so I can see the shape, and I fill the space with something

resembling the oscilloscope trace of an epileptic fit. Sometimes I
know how many words or syllables I need, as well as the stress
formation, so I might write a line as breves and macrons or noughts
and crosses, or I call up similar sounding words or phrases —
cannon fodder — to be sacrificed and replaced at a later stage. On
this basis, my rough notes must look like the jottings of a certifiable
lunatic or a rocket scientist — Paul Newman in that film, chalking
up gobbledygook equations in front of a bamboozled Soviet astro-
physicist.

Finally, I ought to try and say something about the mood of
'Goalkeeper With A Cigarette', and perhaps that of my work in
general. I believe that contemporary poetry makes points about the
universal through observation of the specific and the particular. It's
the case of the insect on the projector lens throwing huge and
terrifying shadows. And I always imagine that area of land between
reader and writer; pitch a poem too close to the author and it's
impenetrable, unfathomable, but push a poem right under a
reader's nose and it's embarrassing, insulting. Poems entitled 'War'
or 'Sorrow' are usually embarking on a one way trip to the waste-
paper basket, but poems that describe the stripping down of a
bolt-action Martini-Henry or an artery of the heart are already half
way towards making a point, and I think as readers of poetry in the
last days of the twentieth century we're too sophisticated to have it
any other way. For the time being, at least.

What follows, then, is an early draft of the poem in question,
followed by the finished or abandoned version. Without the aid of
high-definition xerography I can't reproduce an accurate rendition
of the original workings which tend to consist of over-writing, sub
and super-script and a great many vectors ushering words and
phrases to other coordinates. Imagine Scrabble played on a Snakes
and Ladders board, and you're pretty close. There were twenty-two
pages of drafts in the end, which also included three shopping lists,
several telephone numbers, a hand-drawn map of downtown Kyoto
and an ink slick that continues to feature in the later stages of the
notebook, diminishing on every subsequent page like blood through
a bandage. The draft presented here is sanitized, amalgamated and
typed.

Goalkeeper With A Cigarette

Last of the Smoking Goalkeepers

The Goalkeeper and the Cigarette

Goalkeeper With A Cigarette

That's him in the green jersey/shirt

                       green cotton jersey

           green, green

prince of the clean sheets, some praying mantis

insect, some upright insect

prince of the clean sheets, some upright insect

boxed within the sticks, the horizontal

and the pitch, xo x o x oo x

              behind which the cross-hatching

of the net

              kitted out with skins and flints

                         and a flint

                    Virginia Gold

              that's him again,

rolls his own   already rolled

a packet of twenty tucked up his sleeve

or down one sock   One behind the ear,

flint/skins

dog end

fug

puff

reefer

             with something in/down his sock

and the pitch, with something up his sleeve, armed

with a tin   and skins

and skins for when he rolls his own, a case

containing eight or nine already rolled.

That's him with one tucked out of sight, and lit,

a stamen cupped in the bud of his/the fist.

never refers to himself as a/the cat

but speaks plainly about the onion basket.

That's him, unlike those other clowns

not like those other clowns, limbering up

on the penalty spot, physical jerks

running on the spot and physical jerks

and push or pull or sit ups in the box

around the box and pull ups on the bar

***************lycra pyjama suits

hands   thumbs   all thumbs   fingers

                                          cracked

about as dexterous as a bunch of thumbs

hands that are swaddled and bandaged in gloves

both of them bandaged and xo with gloves

                          in

togged out in - - - pyjama suits

with hands as stunted as a bunch of thumbs,

hands that are swaddled and bandaged with gloves

                  coddled

laughable, frying pan, sausage man gloves?

fingers as crunched   banana man

not a smoking custodian or a keeper

with a fag/bad habit   it's what he does

in one breath saving a penalty with his legs,

taking a deep drag on the goal-line in the next

stub marks on the posts at the pitches where

smoked, butts and stud marks, on the one hand

playing a back-pass with his feet, or *

heading a corner;   corner;

lighting the next from the last in the other.

But not my man, that's not what my man does,
a man who stubs his reefers on the post
                    gaspers
and kicks his heels against stud marks and butts
lighting the next from the last; in one breath
making the save of the day/year with his legs,
taking a deep drag sat on the goal-line/ in the next,
on the one hand throwing out
or fielding a   swirling   corner
                                        other
                            in the cold
                              in the freezing cold
When the team are snorting like horses
                        flogged
when the sweeper talks his game of steaming orders
that's not steam
that's not smoke coming from my bloke, it's smoke.
That's not my man goading the terraces,
bearing his arse to the visitor's end
and dodging the sharpened ten pence pieces
bunce
bunse
cadge
the rest is bunce
no one forced his hand
cadging a light from the stewards and press

police specials

                                                      he is

what he is and does whatever suits him

because he has no \ - \ - song to sing

on the themes of genius or dedication;

in his passport, under occupation

he has written either neither goalie

with a bad habit, nor full time smoker

cum custodian who happens to be

very good at it, or something like it.

Loosing off smoke rings like nobodies business

smoke rings rising nil nil nil

into everyone's faces, up everyone's noses

                                        supposes.

passive thing that no one supposes

above his signature

his signature becomes his autograph

effin' n' jeffin'

highfalutin?   hifalutin?   faluting?

The Faber Book of Modern Thought

zilch   nought

nish

nowt

sweet Fanny Adams   FA

zero   halos

                    his entry reads :

youngsters, young pretenders

*

*

*

take a tip from me/ him and deface yourselves.

                                        wealth

                                        health

better by half to see from the side
better to look from the side at yourselves
better for you to take a sideways view
better for your image and your wealth
think further than your pockets and your health
think further than your pockets, purses, health
think bigger than your pockets, profiles, health

think bigger than your pockets, profiles, health,
better by far to take a side-on/sideways view,
take a tip from me and deface yourselves.

Goalkeeper with a Cigarette

That's him in the green, green cotton jersey,
prince of the clean sheets, some upright insect
boxed between the sticks, the horizontal
and the pitch, stood with something up his sleeve,
armed with a pouch of tobacco and skins
to roll his own, or else a silver tin
containing eight or nine already rolled.
That's him with one behind his ear, between
his lips, or one tucked out of sight and lit -
a stamen cupped in the bud of his fist.
That's him sat down, not like those other clowns,
performing acrobatics on the bar, or press-ups
in the box, or running on the spot,
togged out in turtleneck pyjama-suits
with hands as stunted as a bunch of thumbs,
hands that are bandaged or swaddled with gloves,
laughable, frying-pan, sausage-man gloves.
Not my man, though, that's not what my man does;
a man who stubs his reefers on the post
and kicks his heels in the stud-marks and butts,
lighting the next from the last, in one breath
making the save of the year with his legs,
taking back a deep drag on the goal-line
in the next; on the one hand throwing out
or snaffling the ball from a high corner,

flicking off loose ash with the other. Or
in the freezing cold with both teams snorting
like flogged horses, with captains and coaches
effing and jeffing at backs and forwards,
talking steam, screaming exhausting orders,
that's not breath coming from my bloke, it's smoke.
Not him either goading the terraces,
bearing his arse to the visitor's-end
and dodging the sharpened ten-pence pieces,
playing up, picking a fight, but that's him
cadging a light from the ambulance men,
loosing off smoke rings, zeros or halos
that drift off, passively, over the goals
into nobodies face, up nobodies nose.
He is what he is, does whatever suits him,
because he has no highfalutin song
to sing, no neat message for the nation
on the theme of genius or dedication;
in his passport, under "occupation",
no one forced the man to print the word
"custodian", and in <u>The Faber Book</u>
<u>of Handy Hints</u>, his five line entry reads:
"You young pretenders, keepers of the nought,
the nish, defenders of the sweet fuck-all,
think bigger than your pockets, profiles, health;
better by half to take a sideways view,
take a tip from me and deface yourselves."

Michael Longley
A Tongue At Play

1

At primary school in Belfast we learned by heart poems and passages from the Bible. I enjoyed this, but my chief pleasures were parsing and analysis at which I was a virtuoso, and writing essays. In Form III at grammar school I was moved by Keats's 'La Belle Dame' and de La Mare's 'The Listeners', and that year chose Yeats's *Collected Poems* as my prize for English — which caused some consternation and embarrassment at home. This awakening coincided with my discovery of Grieg, Tchaikovsky, Chopin. Poetry and listening to music come together at deep levels most days of my life. In the Sixth Form our English teacher, Joe Cowan, cyclostyled poems by W.R. Rodgers and Louis MacNeice who, literally, brought poetry home to us. "Is the man a poet?" Joe would chortle, slapping his knee. "I should say so! I should say so!" Such spontaneity was a relief after stammering through Catullus and the *Agamemnon*, the snail's-pace at which adolescence approaches love elegy and tragic chorus. Two essays, 'A Retired Sea Captain' and 'The Family Photograph Album', were published in *School News*. This meant as much to me as keeping my place on the rugby team. At sixteen I fell in love and to impress my girlfriend, wrote my first bad poems. Poetry is still for me a sexy activity.

The creative urge did not take over completely until I went to Dublin in 1958 to study Classics at Trinity College. In that leisurely atmosphere I produced several splurges every day for a year or more without even realising there might be formal problems. By the time I was good enough to have some tiny lyrics accepted by the undergraduate literary magazine *Icarus*, Derek Mahon breezed in from Belfast to unsettle my fragile sense of myself as a "college poet". In his inspiring company I inhaled MacNeice, Graves, Hart Crane, Yeats, Donne, George Herbert, Lowell, Larkin, Hughes, D.H. Lawrence. While I was still a student the *Irish Times* published 'The Flying Fish' and paid me £5 for it, my first literary earnings, an endorsement which helped me believe the rows of words were worth something. I was now addicted to poetry and tottered, a lapsed Classicist, towards a mediocre degree. After a couple of detours I returned to Belfast because my wife-to-be, Edna Broderick, had been appointed lecturer in English at Queen's University. I met Seamus Heaney and his fiancée, Marie Devlin. We all became friends. Those were intense, courageous, competitive times. Poems were exchanged, then praised or condemned. At no stage did we think of ourselves as a school or group, or as "Ulster Poets". Serving my apprenticeship alongside Mahon and Heaney, I learned quickly. There was nothing cosy about our friendships. Although intensely aware of one another's work, we never hunted in a pack.

My first collection *No Continuing City* was turned down by nearly a dozen publishers, often with three or six months between disappointments. Each time it came back I substituted stronger new poems for weaker old ones. When it was published by Macmillan in 1969, I was thirty and the book as sturdy as I was ever likely to make it. I had long been preoccupied with form — pushing a shape as far as it would go, exploring its capacities to control and its tendencies to disintegrate. My poems were getting shorter and shorter. I sensed that the last few to be included in *No Continuing City* were closed circuits. They had about them an air of "end of the road" rather than "en route", and enjoyed already the brevity of epitaphs. The next stage in logical progression would be a blank page and silence. Through 1967 and 1968 I slowed to a stop and became so depressed that I gave up my job as a schoolteacher in order to devote the next year to sorting myself out. My muse did not come on sabbatical with me. Dead silence. Now I didn't even have an alibi. I kept trying, but it wasn't until 1972 that I started to write again with confidence.

I feared that I had nothing more to say. The crisis had probably more to do with the exhaustion of forms than lack of subject matter. I needed new shapes and rhythms. 'Journey out of Essex', subtitled 'John Clare's Escape from the Madhouse', the only poem from 1968 to survive, is more relaxed and conversational than most of the work in *No Continuing City* and it doesn't rhyme. Three to four years later I at last began to register its message in the freer poems of my second volume. I wrote steadily through the nineteen-seventies and enjoyed my new job at the Arts Council of Northern Ireland. In 1979 my fourth book, *The Echo Gate*, was published. A fifth was not to appear until 1991. "This middle stretch of life is bad for poets," MacNeice writes. My second crisis, a decade long and with only fleeting remissions, could be explained in terms of the male menopause and loss of bureaucratic innocence in an increasingly fractious institution. In 1985 I had published *Poems 1963-1983*, which brought together all I wanted to preserve from my four previous collections, plus an ominously short section of new work. Perhaps preparing this premature 'collected' made me too self-aware. It was as though I had drawn a circle in the sand and, transfixed at the centre, could not step outside it. Once again there were formal problems. I attempted to solve these by further prosodic loosenings-up and an increasingly ambitious, even reckless, syntactical reach. My early retirement from the Arts Council at the end of March 1991 coincided to the day with the publication of *Gorse Fires*. The long wait taught me that silence is part of the enterprise.

2

I believe in the old-fashioned notion of inspiration, the breathing into the mind of some idea, the suggestion of an emotion or impulse from outside the confines of your own body and personality. I live for those moments when language itself takes over the enterprise, and insight races ahead of knowledge. Occasionally I have things to say, or there is something I want to describe. But these are not my main reasons for writing. Although it may require much hard work and will-power to finish a poem, I have never started one as an act of will and successfully completed it. Poetry is like a mote in the eye. If you try to focus on it too hard, it disappears. If you desire it too urgently, it may well reject you. No matter how intense the concentration or lofty the ambition, insouciance seems to be a necessary ingredient.

A poem begins as a baby begins. Two cells come together, then multiply and grow. The cells may be ideas, emotions, images, words, rhythmic pulses. Several winters ago the door of our coal-hole dropped off. Heavy snow swirled on to the coal. In order to stoke the fire, we had to carry into the house shovelfuls of coal *and* snow. Burning snow seemed an odd activity. I tossed the image to the back of my mind in the hope that it might one day generate a poem. Months later I spotted in our garden a blackbird with a fleck of white on its plumage. That fleck reminded me of the last traces of snow after a thaw:

> Snow curls into the coalhouse, flecks the coal.
> We burn the snow as well in bad weather
> As though to spring-clean that darkening hole.
> The thaw's a blackbird with one white feather.

Many of my poems have their beginnings in ordinary domestic

experience. (Though nothing remains ordinary if you look at it for long enough. Anyone's back garden can become a gold mine. Poetry is a normal human activity, its concerns all of the things that happen to people.) A poem may lie buried like a shattered vase waiting to be reconstructed. Chance leads you to the fragments which you relate to each other and piece together. I found in a book of old photographs a picture of a woman sewing among the stooks of barley at harvest time. She had carried her basket into the fields, and brought the indoors outdoors, turned her world inside out or outside in (the reverse of snow in the living room). Later I read how in those days sticky goose-grass was used to trawl the churns of milk for cow-hairs. This lead me to the notion of an absent lover's stray hairs in the milk. Then I noticed the long hairs on the heads of barley:

> When barley weighs the food in its hair
> You materialise like a farmer's wife
> Who last summer occupied the distance
> — A sewing basket among the stooks —
> And left me behind, trawling the milk
> With goose-grass for strands of your hair.

Catalogues which release the power of names simply by stringing them together to make rhythmic sense are at the heart of poetry and go all the way back to the catalogue of ships in Homer s *Iliad*. When the man who worked at our local ice-cream shop was murdered by paramilitaries, my younger daughter bought with her ice-cream money a bouquet of carnations to lay on the pavement outside his shop. This happened while I was away from home looking for wild flowers in the Burren in County Clare. Sarah who enjoyed reciting the various flavours, gave me the idea of turning into a wreath of words, a prayer of sorts, the flower names I had jotted down. I worked as hard on this catalogue of flowers as I have on anything:

> Rum and raisin, vanilla, butter-scotch, walnut, peach:
> You would rhyme off the flavours. That was before
> They murdered the ice-cream man on the Lisburn Road
> And you bought carnations to lay outside his shop.
> I named for you all the wild flowers of the Burren
> I had seen in one day: thyme, valerian, loosestrife,
> Meadowsweet, tway blade, crowfoot, ling, angelica,
> Herb robert, marjoram, cow parsley, sundew, vetch,
> Mountain avens, wood sage, ragged robin, stitchwort,
> Yarrow, lady's bedstraw, bindweed, bog pimpernel.

A catalogue like this one is meant to go on for ever. I often scribble down lists of things. Each of the four quatrains of my poem 'Trade Winds' consists mainly of a short catalogue: the names of the locks on the River Lagan, of apples from County Armagh, of clay pipes manufactured in Carrickfergus, and of fishing smacks in Portavogie harbour. The last of these allowed me to say as much about life and death in twenty-four words as I am ever likely to manage in so confined a space. The skippers who had magically christened their boats gave me the poem. Naming anything well is a poetic act:

> Among the Portavogie prawn-fishermen
> Which will be the ship of death: Trade Winds,
> Guiding Starlight, Halcyon, Easter Morn,
> Liberty, Faithful Promise, Sparkling Wave?

Poetry is mainly about putting the right word in the right place, a question of rhythm more than anything else. The ideal choice of word also decides tone of voice and verbal colour. This is where the idiomatic nature of English is valuable. We can further enrich the argot by turning to dialect, though as someone who speaks fairly standard English I would only do so when the dialect of my region, Ulster Scots, sets free a concept or phrase or line which would otherwise not be accessible to me. I had long hoped to make a self-contained lyric out of the scene in Book XXII of the *Odyssey* where Phemios the bard and Medon the herald beg for mercy from Telemachos and his father Odysseus who have just finished slaughtering the suitors. I wanted this to be frightening and funny, but not in a pantomimic way. In his supplication Phemios cajoles and boasts. By serendipity or subconscious design I found myself leafing through an Ulster Scots dictionary. I was reminded that *bam* means to boast, *banny* to cajole. Phemios dashes towards Odysseus and clasps him by the knees. A few page-flicks later I chanced on Ulster Scots words which fitted his actions: *ram-stam* and *grammel*. The four words together made bagpipe music. Even at so early a stage I sensed that I had successfully kidnapped Phemios and Medon from their epic surroundings. In my lyric, Phemios, the self-important bard,

> Makes a ram-stam for Odysseus, grammels his knees,
> Then bannies and bams wi this highfalutin blether ...

There is often a moment in a poem which like a goldsmith's hallmark proves, if only to the poet himself, that he might have created something authentic. In 'Phemios & Medon' the hallmark is a pun which highlights the grim paradox of cleansing through bloodshed. In his slaughter of the suitors Odysseus has splattered blood everywhere. When he talks about cleaning up, I give him the Ulster Scots word for this activity: *redd*. Although I believe that such words should be decipherable and work on their own within context and without a gloss, it pleases me to imagine a reader somewhere far from Ulster finding out what they mean by going back to Homer. The long way home. In the last six lines of my version Odysseus addresses Medon:

> 'You may thank Telemachos for this chance to wise up
> And pass on the message of oul dacency. Go out
> And sit in the haggard away from this massacre,
> You and the well-spoken poet, while I redd the house.'
> They hook it and hunker fornenst the altar of Zeus,
> Afeard and skelly-eyed, keeking everywhere for death.

Hallmarks relate more often than not to formal matters. When I was translating an elegy of Tibullus which I called 'Peace', its argument and movement suggested a shape. I divided my version into ten line stanzas, although the Latin is continuous and does not add up to a multiple of ten. In order to earn the hallmark of a ten line final stanza, I needed to risk the failure of ending up with the wrong number. More recently I worked in much the same way with the story of Baucis and Philemon from Ovid's *Metamorphoses*, except that this time I translated from the end of the poem to the beginning and placed my bet on a five line stanza. When I was a bureaucrat I occasionally wrote poems at my office desk. 'Options' from my second collection was unveiling itself in thirteen line stanzas. I had worked out the first three and in the usual jumble of words and crossings-out was getting down on paper what instinct told me was the substance of a fourth. But a busy colleague interrupted me and kept me from the poem until the office closed. Driving home I said over to myself what was taking shape in my head as the last stanza, and I prayed that it would fall naturally into thirteen lines. At home I scribbled it out and, when I counted thirteen lines, felt exhilaration, relief, gratitude. In the words of another poem, 'Ars Poetica':

> I am writing a poem at the office desk
> Or else I am forging business letters —
> What I am really up to, I suspect,

Is seducing the boss's secretary
Among the ashtrays on the boardroom table
Before absconding with the petty-cash box
And a one-way ticket to Katmandu.

On rare occasions you "find" a poem. In *The Penguin Book of Chinese Verse* I read this lovely 'Drinking Song' by Shen Hsun who lived in the ninth century and was murdered together with his wife by a slave (which lends the poem a strange appropriateness):

Shoot not the wild geese from the south;
Let them northward fly.
When you do shoot, shoot the pair of them,
So that the two may not be put asunder.

I flicked over a few pages and was drawn — inevitably perhaps — to 'The Wild Geese' by Lu Kuei-Meng:

From South to North, how long is the way!
Between them lie ten thousand bows and arrows.
Who can say, through the mist and fog,
How many birds can reach Heng-yang?

By the time I had discovered in the notes that Heng-yang, also called the Turning Geese Peak, is traditionally the southern limit of the migration of the wild geese, simple rhymes were sounding in my ears and reshaping the original translations by Robert Kotewall and Norman L. Smith. I couldn't have written this poem without the effort and the gift of rhyme. My title, 'Chinese Whispers', is meant to suggest how the poem was transmitted to me as well as the *sotto voice* conversation I have invented for two poets whose gentle anxiety is unlikely to save the geese:

'From the south it's a long way
With wildfowlers lying in wait.
How many geese will make it
Through the mist, no-one can say.'

'Don't shoot the last to migrate
From the south: let them fly north.
If you do shoot, shoot them both,
So they won't have to separate.'

People ask awkward questions at poetry readings. One old chestnut is: "Why doesn't your poetry [*or* Modern Poetry] rhyme?". My response is to read out a poem of my own like 'Thaw' or 'Chinese Whispers', and then shift attention from myself by naming some great modern poets who are consummate exponents of rhyme: Yeats, Auden, MacNeice, Frost. A lot of modern poetry, I insist, does rhyme. My own gifted contemporaries, Seamus Heaney and Derek Mahon, work with equal ease in free forms and in stricter conventional stanzas that use rhyme-schemes. A younger Ulster poet, Paul Muldoon, has taken the art of rhyme to new heights of subtlety and sophistication. A virtuoso deployment of rhyme has been a feature of Northern Irish poetry for more than three decades. Every line in my own first collection rhymes. I now rhyme only occasionally. Rhyme is one of the things that words do. In as much as poetry takes advantage of all of those things, I regret not using rhyme more frequently (though receptive always to assonance, its clashes and chimes). When asked where he got his ideas from, Yeats sounded as though he was joking, but he was in fact hinting at a mystery: "Looking for the next rhyme," he replied. The search for a rhyme resembles drilling for water which natural pressure then raises to the surface, an artesian well. The poet drills down through strata of language and memory to release what seems to have been waiting there all along. In my poem 'She-wolf' one lovely obsolete word licenced me to express tender feelings through almost ridiculous rhymes. "Nuddle" means "to push with the nose" but it also combines "nuzzle" and "cuddle", and conjures up the contented fug of cubs or pups in their den. Its two syllables and the rhymes they attract make the poem:

> Fingers and toes, a tail wagging,
> And there in the middle
> Rome like a sore belly-button
> Peeps out from the huddle.
>
> She licks Romulus and Remus
> The moment they piddle,
> Her cold nose tickling the heads
> That nod off and nuddle.

The presence of rhyme does not prove that a piece of writing is poetry. The rhymes that generate the sad jangle and mechanical thump of obituary notices and birthday verses are lipstick on the corpse of dead language. The gap between verse and poetry is enormous. Between good poetry and good prose the gap is much narrower. What they have in common is vitality of rhythm. Poetry's

only crucial attribute is rhythm. This is its heart-beat. This makes
it memorable. If the rhythm falters, then the poem dies of heart-failure.
Rhyme helps to promote the rhythm of a poem, but it is not
essential. The only way to find out if a poem is alive or dead is to
read it aloud. Most poets (and I am no exception) can he heard
mumbling to themselves as they write. When you read good poetry
aloud, your lips pout and stretch, your tongue jives, your whole
mouth is vigorously exercised. In a verse letter I describe poetry as
"a tongue at play / With lip and tooth". We launch poetry from our
mouths. It finds its resting place in our ears, and in our memories.
This is not just an individual but also a communal process. Poetry
has been defined as "memorable speech". Better to be remembered
for a couplet than forgotten for epics. Robert Frost said he wanted
to lodge a few poems where they could not be got rid of.

Writing a poem is an experiment, an exploration. You do not
know beforehand what you are going to say. If you do, you are
merely versifying opinion. A poet on the track of the real thing will
find himself in unknown territory, using the form of the poem (as
it emerges) as an explorer uses compass and sextant. Poetry is an
inner adventure. My poem 'Ars Poetica' plays with these ideas. Here
is the fourth section:

> After I've flown my rickety bi-plane
> Under the Arc de Triomphe and before
> I perform a double back-somersault
> Without the safety net and — if there's time —
> Walk the high wire between two waterfalls,
> I shall draw a perfect circle free-hand
> And risk my life in a final gesture.

I imply that poetry can he a hazardous business. The playful tone
is necessary because the real subject of 'Ars Poetica' is the shadowy
territory at the back of the mind where nightmares and phobias lurk:

> Someone keeps banging the side of my head
> Who is well aware that it's his furore,
> His fists and feet I most want to describe —
> My silence to date neither invitation
> Nor complaint, but a stammering attempt
> Once and for all to get him down in words
> And allow him to push an open door.

Poetry composed at any psychological depth can be as dangerous
as walking a tightrope or rock-climbing. Technique is vital. If many

of the talentless, careless folk who call themselves poets were
tightrope-walkers, they would be dead. I like Ezra Pound's equating
of an artist's technique with his sincerity. Horace calls the poet
musarum sacerdos, priest of the muses. The Scottish word *makar* is
a straight translation of the Greek *poetes*. The poet oscillates between
notions of craft and vision. If he settles too long for one or the other,
he becomes boring. Ideally plan and passion, improvisation and
calculation coincide. When I was a student of Classics at Trinity
College Dublin, the Professor of Greek, W.B. Stanford who was
taking us through Aristotle's *Poetics*, asked us to bring to the next
seminar our own definitions of poetry. Mine was (and is): "If prose
is a river, poetry is a fountain". The form of a poem acts like the
nozzle through which water is forced under pressure to make shapes
in the air. Poems and fountains exist as shapes which stay the same
by changing (or which change by staying the same).

3

Last year I read my poems to schoolchildren in one of Belfast's more
tumultuous areas. I thought they would have seen and heard enough
about the Troubles and chose some of my more peaceable poems
— love poems, poems about nature. During question time I was
asked: "Mr Longley, do you have any political opinions what-
soever?" "Why do you ask?" "Well to judge from what you've been
reading this afternoon, you seem to be walking around in a romantic
haze!" I do have political opinions, I insisted, and I have written
poems which deal directly with the Troubles. A poem's weight and
seriousness should not however be measured by its subject matter
alone. A bad poem about the hydrogen bomb tells us infinitely less
than a good poem about a blackbird. That is one side of the
argument. In 1979 I wrote in the *Poetry Book Society Bulletin* about
what I was trying to do in my fourth collection *The Echo Gate*:
"Though the poet's first duty must be to his imagination, he has
other obligations — and not just as a citizen. He would be inhuman
if he did not respond to tragic events in his own community, and a
poor artist if he did not seek to endorse that response imaginatively.
But if his imagination fails him the result will be a dangerous
impertinence. In the context of political violence the deployment of
words at their most precise and suggestive remains one of the few
antidotes to death-dealing dishonesty." I have written a few inade-
quate elegies. I offer them as wreaths. That is all.

I write for everyone and for no one in particular. The first person I try to please is myself. A poem is an organism in which relationships on many levels between words fuse various orders of experience into a unique perception. A poet makes the most complex and concentrated response that can be made with words to the total experience of living. For these reasons I would go on trying to write poems, even if nobody wanted to read them.

Gillian Clarke
The King of Britain's Daughter

An architect said, "I see a vision. I can't see the building yet. No lines, no walls. Only space and light". That's how it feels when a poem is about to form: there is excitement, a blurred image and not quite discernible lines, but the form has yet to emerge. Even if there are words it is too dark to read them, though a phrase or a line may be legible already. However, the moment this unclear vision declares its presence one can be certain that the poem can be written.

For me, the poem arrives in a coinciding moment of language and energy. Its subject is like a novelist's plot — merely an excuse to rummage in the mind for language. There are few plots and all writers share the same small store, using them over and over again. When a poem is on the way it feels as though energy has been lying in wait for language. Or is it the other way about? And whence does that language come flooding, as strongly as any of the driving human passions, and as suddenly, as mysteriously? The poem is begun in that moment of germination, though it must be unmade and made again in the cold light of the mind before it can be called a finished work of art. To have an *idea* for a poem is to have nothing at all.

In 1990, at the first of the Hay-on-Wye Literary Festival weekend "Squantums", the plot offered to six poets late on Friday evening was 'Border: Fatherland, Motherland'. What I saw at once was that border country in the self where mother and father meet, an edge where there is both tension and conflict. At the same time it was the border where the two languages of Wales define themselves and each other, and the definition of self and other was one of the most intriguing aspects of the subject. The meaning of border deepened, layer by layer. I saw those borders inside Wales like a backwards journey into history where the post-industrial south dwindles among tin sheds and tethered alsatians, where sad ponies starve on the yellowed grass of slag, and where, one ridge onwards, another Wales begins as a mountain tilts westward into pasture and wooded valleys. Somewhere in this complex mental landscape of fractures and sutures a childhood tilts into adulthood. The poem I want to discuss was prompted by that moment. But before I can arrive at that poem, I should return to the place whence I think it came, and try to chart its long progress.

The Irish sea breaks on the shores of my father's land of Dyfed, specifically a small stretch of north Pembrokeshire. We are walking the beach. My father is a great story-teller, and today he tells me the story of Branwen and Bendigeidfran, the children of Llŷr, explaining to his young daughter, mythologically, historically and geologically, two features of the coast close to my grandmother's farm, known as Fforest. One is a vast rocking stone, or logan-stone, probably Neolithic, balanced on the cliff and visible from the farmhouse. It is, according to my father, the giant Bendigeidfran's apple, or sometimes his pebble, as the story is ever-changing. The other is a black rock-pool vaguely the shape of a footprint and as big as a bath, which fills with sea water at high tide. It is, my father tells me, a footprint burnt into the shore by the enraged Bendigeidfran, setting off for Ireland to rescue Branwen from her cruel life as the rejected wife of the Irish king.

As a child I used to play a game which I called "big and little", which now seems to me a primitive version of a poet's game, physical and imaginative in nature, yet a child's way into a questioning habit of thought. Half-close your eyes and stare, or blur your ears. A stone becomes a planet. Your breath is the wind, a quarrel is a storm, a storm becomes a war. It works the other way too. Your cupped hand can balance the pebble of the setting sun before it is dropped into the sea. With a finger you can blot out a Neolithic stone, or a planet. Take a magnifying glass to your thumb-print. Place a hair under a microscope. These are geographies. It is a game played with scale and perspective that has always fascinated me. It prepared me for the theory, later encountered when I began to study Shakespeare, of man as microcosm, the epitome of the macrocosmic universe.

A poem can be a long time coming. Mine often send signals decades before they arrive. I first "studied" Shakespeare seriously for A level but by then I had often been taken to the theatre and was sufficiently familiar with more than a dozen of the plays to find the characters and their language entering my dreams. I knew passages by heart. I had Lawrence Olivier's autograph. I had seen his spittle glitter on the air when, as Titus Andronicus, he hissed "because I have no more tears to shed" in a whisper that carried to every ear in the house. Theatre was the most glamorous source of stories that I knew.

Of all the plays it was *King Lear* which first and most powerfully touched the fiction of my own inner life. At ten years old I was taken to see the play at Stratford-on-Avon by one of my father's three sisters, an aunt who was no scholar, merely a railway clerk with a love of books. Soon afterwards she took me to *The Tempest*. They

seemed familiar dramas, these father and daughter plays set in a
damp Atlantic Ocean past in which I felt I stood and walked and
spoke, and had my own part to play. In a recurring dream of
childhood I'm walking by the sea and someone is whispering, "The
isle is full of noises".

From my infancy Europe had been at war, and the theatre of war,
as far as I could understand it, was the radio. My father was a
broadcasting engineer with the BBC, so there were radios in every
room. The radio on the ocean-facing windowsill at Fforest was a
teller of wild tales that came straight off the Irish Sea, as did the rain
and the wind and the refracted light of the setting sun. These were
stories of a great enemy who must be killed so that we could all be
safe again. My father's radio was the voice of the story-teller. Later,
when I was ten, I was to hear Shakespeare's words, and would at
once know they were describing the "sounds and sweet airs" of
Fforest. It was not difficult to imagine my grandmother's farm as
an isle full of noises, cut off by the sea, poor roads, weather and the
family from bombs, sirens and air raids, though not from the
rumours of war. Life into language equals fiction.

It was that complex experience of real life tangled with the life of
the imagination that lay in wait for the language I was to hear that
first time at the Memorial Theatre, Stratford. To two connecting
stories I already knew — the story of Branwen, and my own — was
added the story of Lear, which came in words so awesomely
mysterious that I was to remember fragments of it forever. It would
enter the ground of my mind, along with hymns, and passages of
the King James translation of the Bible regularly repeated just as
theatrically in Chapel. I was an early reader, and I entered books at
an age when it is natural to confuse the real world with the world of
literature, the self with the characters in stories. Thus, alongside
nursery rhymes, "the moon doth shine as bright as day", or "the
man in the wilderness said to me", playground games, "Poor Mary
is a-weeping", biblical language such as "tell it not in Gath, publish
it not on the streets of Escalon", and the great Welsh hymns, "Dyma
cariad fel y moroedd", "here is love like the sea", or the hauntingly
simple poetry of "there is a green hill far away", came the equally
strange and beguiling spells of Shakespeare, spells such as "Nothing
will come of nothing. Speak again". I have not, nor will I check these
quotations from the Bible, the hymn book, and from Shakespeare.
This is how I remember them. This is how the words must stay,
even, perhaps, in misquotation. Those words, in that order, are a
part of the "fiction" I have been writing all my life.

The earliest poem-harbinger of 'The King of Britain's Daughter', as far as I can see, was a poem called 'Llŷr', written almost fifteen years ago. It was commissioned by the late Sam Wanamaker for one of his series of anthologies, *Poems for Shakespeare*. 'Llŷr' recalls the earliest ecstatic moment of my own experience of Shakespeare's spellbinding power. It carries hints that I was in thrall to language, like many children, from the first lullaby, the first nursery rhyme, the first hymn, the first playground chant. Llŷr, King of Britain, is Lear, and my father, and he will later hand on his role in my mind to his son, Bendigeidfran (the brother I never had), or Bran, to give him his shorter name, although there is no hint of that story in the poem 'Llŷr'. I am Cordelia, and if Cordelia is the daughter of Llŷr, she must also be Branwen. So it was that, without knowing it at the outset, I embarked on the ambitious project of a long poem about childhood in a time of war, with *The Bible, The Mabinogion, The Complete Works of Shakespeare*, and a book of nursery rhymes in hand.

In the poem 'Llŷr', precursor of the later sequence, I use the landscape of Llŷn in Gwynedd, where I happened to be staying when I wrote it.

> Ten years old, at my first Stratford play:
> The river and the king with their Welsh names
> Bore in the darkness of a summer night
> Through interval and act and interval.
> Swans moved double through glossy water
> Gleaming with imponderable meanings.
> Was it Gielgud on that occasion?
> Or ample Laughton, crazily white-gowned,
> Pillowed in wheatsheaves on a wooden cart,
> Who taught the significance of little words?
> All. Nothing. Fond. Ingratitude. Words
> To keep me scared, awake at night. That old
> Man's vanity and a daughter's 'Nothing',
> Ran like a nursery rhythm in my head.

It is no accident that I chose the fourteen line stanza and, more or less, iambic pentameter. The formal use of capitals initialling each line now looks old-fashioned to me. I abandoned a stiffer earlier draft using regular rhyme, though the chiming within the poem is important to it, and deliberate. The remembered performance by Charles Laughton is substantiated by others, and I believe it to be the one which mainly influenced the description in Leon Garfield's 'King Lear' in his version of Shakespeare's stories,

> a mad, wild old man, stuck all over with wild flowers, and
> crowned with weeds,

and later,

> Gentle hands had taken him, and tended him, and washed
> him, and put him in fine soft clothes.
> (*Shakespeare Stories*, Leon Garfield)

The evidence of obsessions that would later be developed in 'The
King of Britain's Daughter' can be drawn from hints that lie in the
poem 'Llŷr': "the significance of little words", the list of the words
which Shakespeare plays with in the drama, and "a daughter's
'Nothing', / ran like a nursery rhythm in my head".

Rereading the next stanza now, I am surprised and pleased to see
the image of the bruise in the sea, a metaphor which, by the time I
wrote 'The King of Britain's Daughter', I had forgotten I had used
before. I see no reason to avoid repeating the natural and instinctive
use of such an image, since it is the thread of unity holding poem
to poem, book to book. In 'Llŷr' the description of the height of the
cliffs comes from Shakespeare, as well as from personal observation
of looking down at the sea from the cliffs of Llŷn,

> I watch how Edgar's crows and choughs still measure
> How high cliffs are, how thrown stones fall
> Into history, how deeply the bruise
> Spreads in the sea where the wave has broken.
>   ('Llŷr')

Shakespeare puts it this way,

> How fearful
> And dizzy 'tis to cast one's eyes so low!
> The crows and choughs that wing the midway air
> Show scarce so gross as beetles,

and fifteen years after 'Llŷr' I wrote,

> On the headland is an absence
> where it fell some winter night
> between here and childhood,
> and the sea's still fizzing
> over a bruise that will not heal.
>   ('King of Britain's Daughter')

Although the cliffs I experienced as a child were real cliffs, it was when the experience met the language of Shakespeare that I knew how to feel their height. It was the language of poetry that turned the dizzy view from a cliff-top into a whole experience, from a vertigo of the body into a vertigo of the mind and the imagination.

'Llŷr' links other aspects of the Lear memory with the future King of Britain poem: "figures of old men", "the bearded sea", and "guilty daughters". The last stanza submits to an irregular, perhaps an eccentric rhyme scheme:

> Night falls on Llŷn, on forefathers,
> Old Celtic kings and the more recent dead,
> Those we are still guilty about, flowers
> Fade in jam jars on their graves; renewed
> Refusals are heavy on our minds.
> My head is full of sound, remembered speech,
> Syllables, ideas just out of reach;
> The close, looped sound of curlew and the far
> Subsidiary roar, cadences shaped
> By the long coast of the peninsula,
> The continuous pentameter of the sea.
> When I was ten a fool and a king sang
> Rhymes about sorrow, and there I heard
> That nothing is until it has a word.

That "nothing" unconsciously stolen from Shakespeare has become, I suppose, the absence on the cliff, the fallen stone, the father who died, which I will explain when I discuss the 'King of Britain's Daughter'.

The storm in *Lear* is almost one of the characters in the play. Weather is a ready metaphor, and winters in Pembrokeshire hurled the great Atlantic at the windows of Fforest Farm. Downstairs, family life seethed in a "cawl" comprising, in various combinations at different times, a large cast of characters coming and going about the constant figure of my grandmother. Those exits and entrances were of my father, mother, sister, three aunts, an uncle, and several surrogate uncles who were farm workers. I think of the ash tree lashing the windows in a poem by D.H. Lawrence where downstairs his parents are quarrelling. Not only adult rows, but the babble of downstairs after a child's bedtime, the imperfectly tuned disharmonies of radio, talk, dispute, hint and rumour, send upstairs to the listening child a message that the world is full of tumultuous secrets. Legends made sense of the rumours, as was, I believe, their original purpose, when the earliest story-tellers made metaphors of human

history and psychology in the light of man's understanding of the
world at the time. Both our childhood and our ancestral selves might
see war as a giant, for instance.

Staying at the Smithy, Llanthony, owned in the early nineteenth
century by the poet Walter Savage Landor, on the first day of the
Hay-on-Wye weekend, I began work on my commission. I wrote a
poem under the working title 'The Stone', and at second draft
changed it to 'The Rocking Stone'. Once I had chosen the stone,
already described above, as my symbolic key to the poem which, I
knew, had been lying in wait for decades for its language, it was as
if I had placed it in a sling and swung it hard — and I'm aware here
of the biblical reference to another giant, another stone. 'The
Rocking Stone' moved with its own momentum, or, to use its own
history as a metaphor, once it had rocked too far it lost balance, and
nothing could hold it back. For indeed, by the time the poem was
written the stone had gone. After millennia of erosion it had fallen
at last, in a storm I suppose, to be lost in the depths of the sea at the
foot of the cliffs before I could write about it, although it was
certainly there on the headland throughout my childhood and into
my early twenties.

I took a sheet of paper and wrote: "*Llanthony. 2nd June 1990*. On
the headland is an absence, / where it fell, some winter night /
between here and childhood. Since / I've searched the beach". Then
I crossed out the four lines and tried again. The first sixteen words,
as far as "childhood", remained in every succeeding draft, though
with different line-breaks, until the poem was published in May,
1993.

Not the stone but its absence became the poem's generating
moment, Cordelia's "nothing". My own father had died before I
was twenty. The stone had already left the sling. It was the "airy
nothing" to which I would try to give "a local habitation and a name"
(*Midsummer Night's Dream*). I always wanted a brother, and a
fantasy brother was the next best thing. Was the giant brother
Bendigeidfran/Goliath/father killed by the poem? Can remembered
life survive the fiction we make of it? Is this the purpose and meaning
of elegy?

On the sixth sheet dated 2nd June, is a version of 'The Stone'
which concludes:

> balanced its mass so delicately,
> four thousand years withstanding weather
> like a dozing horse.
>   ('The King of Britain's Daughter')

three lines which remain in every draft until the poem reaches its
completion. The following four lines, which first appear in version
three, contain the exact words of the final published one:

> On the headland is an absence where it fell
> some winter night between here and childhood,
> and the sea's still fizzing
> over a bruise that will not heal.
>   ('The Stone', 3rd version)

The poem then proceeds on an increasingly determined course,
through themes and phrases that will later develop into two whole
and separate poems, the first and third of the final sequence. In draft
four, almost all of both poems are there, tangled together, as the
ideas rush in too fast to sort them out. In a draft written later that
day, seven out of twelve of the lines that will conclude the published
sequence, 'The King of Britain's Daughter', are already written:

> When I took you there,
> a pebble of basalt in my pocket,
> I showed you the white farm, the black beach,
> the empty headland where the stone
> balanced its mass so delicately,
> four thousand years withstanding weather
> like a dozing horse.
>   ('The King of Britain's Daughter')

For the sake of chronology I will return to the other half of the theme
set at Hay — Motherland — and to the other poem I wrote on the
first day. At the time I thought I would write eventually on both
themes, (in fact, I believe I will, in a future book), and that if a long
poem were completed, it would reflect both sides of the border,
because at the time it seemed that the interesting area was the border
itself, the scar, the edge of conflict and healing.

In pursuit of motherland I wrote 'Sunday'. The first image that
came to me was that symbol of marriage and Sunday dinner, the
wedding silver. From that came the golden question mark, the little
hook that locked those old gilded leather cutlery cases, their lids
lined with padded white satin under which bone-handled dinner
and desert knives, two kinds of fork, silver soup and desert spoons
were laid to rest all week in their beds of violet or cobalt velvet,
sometimes "Sylvoed" before being stored. Fish knives and forks,
and tea spoons, were laid in separate boxes.

These are ceremonial objects, and Sunday was a special day.

Many children in those days (the forties and fifties) found their parents' interpretation of these ceremonials differed. For my mother Sunday lunch was the centre-piece. For my father the day's pleasures lay in the freedom of the workshop, in mending and making things. For a child there was, in the air of such a day, such a chance of familiar magic that it must, ultimately, disappoint. To be with the two loved people offers the possibility of joy, maybe an outing, the healing of rifts. But Sunday is also where father, mother and child meet at the border where the fissures and the tensions are. It's where the barbed wire is. It ends in tears, of course.

'Sunday' was written on June 3rd at Llanthony in two hand-written drafts and a typed one. The third draft is almost the same as the one which is published in the collection, *The King of Britain's Daughter*. The house we lived in, from when I was about ten until I was an adult, had a basement. In the first draft I am in that basement, in my father's workshop, and my mother is "upstairs", on the ground floor, "unhooking the golden question mark". In draft two the final version of the first two stanzas is decided, except that the earlier "locked" has become "unlocked", a moment of release instead of entrapment, perhaps. The writing of the poem was an honest journey into remembering, an attempt at the accurate recapturing of detail, the spoons and forks "powdery with Sylvo", the oiled bits of the drill, the colour of the oil. Then I recaught the day's emotions and found the miming cat among the more obvious remembered things, church bells, the smell of sprouts. Poetry is a hook for memory. Out of the excitement of writing emerged, to my surprise, "the small horizon of the water-jug", the connecting looking-glass surfaces of water and mirror that must have remained from the sill and horizon of house and sea I had been preoccupied with in 'The Rocking Stone', and beyond which there was to be found another world. Water and mirror would lead me to the garden pond where I would find, resting at the edge, a stone. It seemed natural, an accurate memory though perhaps not from that particular day, that the child grieving for a spoilt Sunday would lie beside the water with the cat, "inching a stone to edge, until it fell".

Since 'Sunday', the earliest version of 'The Rocking Stone', and the lines which would conclude 'The King of Britain's Daughter' were all written and drafted in the few hours between reporting to an audience eager to know how we were getting on with the task, the writing was interrupted by several public discussions. I recall describing to the audience the surprise I felt at the fall of the stone into the pond. I knew at the time that I was writing about pain and darkness, about a child sulking, but the final line came to me a split second before I could realise that I was foretelling the fall of the logan-stone, the absence on the cliff, and the other absences and "nothings" that the yet unwritten longer poem would contain. I recall taking a quick breath of excitement, a coming up for air, as image and understanding of the image filled me before the ink had dried on the page. At that moment the child in fantasy, and the real child I had been, (for it really did happen), became the storm that pushed a Neolithic boulder into the sea. It was in that moment of connection that the stone gained its full potency as a poet's object of desire, a weapon to slay a foe.

The other symbol to set down its mark here is the horizon, which is to become so important not only in the sequence, but in the whole collection, *The King of Britain's Daughter*. The horizon will be as significant as the stone in the long sequential fatherland poem yet to be written.

> In the salt-blind dining room
> I levelled myself against the small horizon
> of the water jug. The mirrors steadied.

Horizons are about the crossing of oceans, the track of light on the sea, the path into the sunset taken by the Startrite children in an old advertisement, the two little figures in a Charlie Chaplin film, setting off on their adventures, the road through the magical peaks in Rupert Bear books, story-book characters with their bundles on sticks, off to seek their fortunes. I have elsewhere talked of how I saw radio as my first travelling. At a turn of the tuning knob of the radio (which stood on that other horizon, the window sill) I could hear the place-names and languages of faraway places. These glassy levels, horizontals and verticals, are thrown by the wobble of tears in the "salt-blind" dining room.

In the outburst of a first idea, a few hours of work will bring a short poem into being. To develop such an idea into something much more, longer, deeper, more satisfying, something more is needed. I have thought long about this, in order to help others with their writing. The most potent source of energy for me is intense concentration. It sounds so obvious that I wish I could find a more striking word than "concentration", without reaching for terms like "meditation", which suggests something quasi-religious. However, a creative concentration must be deep, uninterruptable, and self-centred. The other useful intellectual tool is research. This could mean reading, or looking, among other things. I would like to broaden the idea of research here. For my purposes I needed factual books, on geology for example, and maps of the coast. There are often verbal treasures to be found in the language of geology, geography, science and technology, a fresh vocabulary and a startling imagery. But I need poetry too, and by broadening the meaning of "research" I include the necessity to read the best poetry in order to write it. Nothing is more inspiring than the work of fine writers. In the early stages of all intense writing periods I carry books around with me, and many of these are poetry books. Beginners often express their fear of imitating other writers, but reading which is sufficient in quantity and richness is nourishing and thrilling. The poet finds a voice to respond to the dialogue of poetry, and will strengthen in eloquence in the excitement of such discourse.

What excited the first words into life in 'The Stone' were the languages I'd heard in childhood, and the possibility of language that spoke from the stone itself. I began to consider the legend, and the metaphor it suggested, the levels of meaning it brought together, the significance it gave to the present. Images moved towards each other. Boulder / skimstone / sun / sand-grain; horizon / sea window-sill; radio / father / voices / stories; war / quarrels / storms. The possibility now occurred to me to connect the many-layered, much-sourced story with the living experience of the present. I felt there was a connection between the brother-sister relationship, of which I had no experience, and the father-daughter relationship which I knew. I would return to Fforest, now, in the present tense, addressing the listener, my companion, telling him the story. This, I decided, would make the poem immediate for myself and for the reader.

In any case there was no avoiding the poem now: the ideas were coming in too fast to record. I would attempt to parallel the legend of Branwen and Bendigeidfran with real life through remembering. I saw art but not artificiality in the idea, since the story of Branwen had been made my own. My father had given it to me. I noted themes for poems as they occurred. A few months after Hay I wrote in my notebook:

> shipwrecks and mysteries; *The Marie Celeste; The Titanic*: photograph of the shark in the ballroom, ships, 'Sparks' officer', [my father had been a merchant ships wireless officer for the Marconi company], Morse code, linking circles, lime kilns, houseboat, Concorde, radios.

Research can always offer a fresh vocabulary, and a map of Pembrokeshire soon yielded rich geological language. I walked the cliffs and beaches again, rediscovering what I thought I had forgotten. I swam out into the bay and around the cliffs, searching for the drowned logan-stone,

> Today I swim beyond the empty headland
> in search of the giant's stone.
> Do I see it through green translucent water,
> shadow of a wreck, a drowned man's shoulder, a clavicle
> huge as a ship's keel wedged between rocks?
> (poem 14, 'The King of Britain's Daughter')

Writing is itself a way to salvage memory. Staring at the page, beginning to set down the first marks, like drawing, and diving under the sea in search for the stone, set going submarine thoughts. Within this undersea which I have elsewhere called the other country ('Seals', *Letting in the Rumour*), lies the archaeology of both the sea-bed and the subconscious. I soon remembered shipwrecks my father had told me about, or about which I had read. There were other forgotten, half-understood things down there, a memory of my mother, for instance, dressed up for a dance, which brought with it an unaccountable sense of loss. The glittering ball-gown merged with a beautiful and famous photographic image of a shark swimming down the staircase into the derelict ballroom of the *Titanic*,

> a staircase in the sea
> and something gleaming in the deepest water.
> (poem 10, 'The King of Britain's Daughter')

I recalled the scientific knowledge my father had shared with me, especially on radio, sound, light, space, the stars. Sometimes, as the BBC Outside Broadcasts Engineer, he took me with him on his site planning visits to chapels, village halls, castles, marquees, even fields. A remembered visit to a chapel set going the poem, 'Radio Engineer' which became poem number 11, and which I believe to be at the heart of 'The King of Britain's Daughter'. I would like to quote it in full.

> i *The Heaviside Layer*

> Staring into the starry sky, that time
> in the darkest dark of war and countryside,
> 'What is the stars?'
> my father asked,

then told me that up there,
somewhere between us and Orion,
hangs the ionosphere, lower, closer at night,
reflecting his long wave signals back to earth,

light bending in water.
But things get tight and close,
words, music, languages
all breathing together under that old carthen,

Cardiff, Athlone, Paris
all tongue-twisted up,
all crackle and interference,
your ears hearing shimmer

like trying to stare at stars.

ii *Bedtime*

You'd plan for it, set out equipped,
warmed in and out before you left the fire
for the dash up the dark stairs.
Hot milk, hot water bottles, coats on the bed.
The quickest way to get warm
was to make yourself small,
to pinch shut the edges
of flannelette, carthen, eiderdown, coats,
to breathe in the stuffy cave till you fell asleep
under the breathless weight of the Heaviside layer,
and woke, stunned, into a crowing light.

iii

With wires, transmitters, microphones,
my father unreeled his line

to cast his singing syllables at the sky,
unleashed and riding airwaves up and up

to touch and be deflected,
moths at a silver window in the air.

I saw it, a cast line falling back
through shaken light above the pool,

sound parting water
like a hare in corn.

iv

Outside in the graveyard
I collected frozen roses,
an alabaster dove with a broken wing
for my hoard in the long grass,

while he unreeled his wires down the aisle,
hitched the microphone to the pulpit
and measured silence with a quick chorus
from The Messiah.

Still I can't look at stars,
or lean with a telescope, dizzy, against the turning earth,
without asking again, 'What is the stars?'
or calling 'Testing, testing' into the dark.

Once that poem was written, I knew that 'The King of Britain's Daughter' would be the elegy for my father I had waited thirty years to write.

In the summer of 1992, a commission came from the Hay-on-Wye Festival for me to work with composer Adrian Williams to make a cantata out of the sequence. I returned to the handful of poems already completed, including 'Radio Engineer', and, with singers in mind, I wrote the deliberately simple and dramatic 'Songs of Branwen' and the 'Lament of Bendigeidfran', and placed them immediately after 'Radio Engineer' in the sequence, thus setting the most important of the personal poems side by side with the legend.

By the time the last stanza of 'Radio Engineer' arrives, I am alone. I am the older generation now that I have no father. His voice testing the microphone and the acoustics of a chapel is my voice shouting at space "Is anybody out there?". The evocatively named Heaviside layer, against which long wave radio signals are bounced, (so named because it was discovered by Professor Heaviside), and the old traditionally woven Welsh wool carthens on the beds in my grandmother's farm, had merged and became metaphors for each other long ago in my mind. My father often quoted from Sean O'Casey's The Plough and the Stars. Gazing up into the night sky and saying, "What is the stars?" was the nearest we, born into a Welsh Baptist tradition but not practising it, got to questioning the mysterious possibility of God. The significance of stars in the dark sky, "in the darkest dark of war and countryside", troubles poem after poem in the sequence. In poem number 9, 'Giants', Bendigeidfran is back, but this time he is stamping his raging foot not on a rocky shore, but in space, bringing together legend and late twentieth century technology, making myth out of breaking the sound-barrier:

> Tonight, as Concorde folds her tern-wings back
> to take the Atlantic,
> I hear a giant foot stamp twice.
> You can still see the mark he made,
> a black space in the stars.

Bendigeidfran's footprint has become a negative, a space where nothing is. When I first read aloud to myself the final lines of 'Radio Engineer', I felt dizzy at what the words were telling me. I had been aiming for a simple language, and to curb my natural extravagance with words. I had hoped to cut a clean syntax out of stone and horizon, to purge my work of adjectives and adverbs. For a writer the language is everything and everything is in the language. Ideas follow language. Symbolism collects about it. Metaphor speaks through it. The horizon is the water-table of 'Anorexic', (a poem in the collection *The King of Britain's Daughter*, but outside the sequence). It is a window-sill, water-table, the surface of the sea, the ionosphere, the lateral gossamer of a spiders web. "The rising sun / on the wall like a crock of marigolds", in the castle of Branwen's exile in Ireland, refers, without first asking my permission, to a jar of marigolds on the farm windowsill of Fforest. Then it becomes the legendary apple, turns into a pebble of amber, to the game called skimstones, to all stones. It is, being a rising sun, the stone redis-covered, the hot star by which we live. Likewise, without asking me, in the closing lines of poem 16 which concludes the sequence, language hands me a stone,

> Walking the beach
> we felt the black grains give
> and the sun stood
> one moment on the sea
> before it fell.

Vicki Feaver
The Handless Maiden

An exercise I often set students is to describe someone doing or making something. It has produced marvellous poems, from a father cleaning the family's shoes, lining them up regimentally, brown on one side of the table, black on the other, to a grandmother polishing the silver sugar bowl her dead husband was presented after fifty years as an insurance clerk.

When I set myself the same exercise I wrote about my mother making crab apple jelly, describing how after the long process of extracting the juice from the fruit and boiling it up with sugar, she held up to the light a jar that was "the colour of fire".

I can see now, though I don't think I thought of it at the time, why it was so important to me. The crab apple trees grew wild in the lanes near the field where my parents kept their caravan. Come August the branches were crowded with sour red apples. My mother couldn't bear to let such bounty go to waste.

It is the same motive that spurs me to write poems. I write, above all, to preserve things, as if I were stocking a larder. For me, the writing of every poem that isn't just a pretence of a poem is like making that jelly: a boiling down of the essence until the moment, so risky and difficult to judge, so open to the possibility of failure, when it can be poured into a jar and left to cool and set.

There have been long periods when I haven't written. As a small child, I sewed together sheets of Jeyes toilet paper to make a book and wrote poems, or what I thought were poems, on the thin brown pages. I said I wanted to be a poet. But there my creativity stopped. Required, aged nine, to write a poem for school homework (this was before the days of Ted Hughes's *Poetry in the Making*, of Poets in Schools, of teachers using poetry to reinforce rather than undermine a child's confidence), I copied out "Up the airy mountain, Down the rushy glen". At fourteen, I put together a sonnet by cannibalising lines from Shakespeare's sonnets. (This is not something I would advise. Both my attempts at plagiarism resulted in humiliating public denunciation.)

To write a poem was too daunting. Yet I was still secretly obsessed with the idea of being a poet. I stole a beautiful, blue, cloth covered edition of Blake's *Songs of Innocence and Experience* from my parents' bookcase and kept it under my bed, along with a red and gold and completely out-dated medical dictionary. At night, I read alternately

"Ah Sunflower, weary of time" and "O Rose, thou are sick" and the symptoms of hysteria and tuberculosis.

My mother insists I had poems in the school magazine. All I have been able to find is a faintly erotic prose piece about fish swimming between my legs on a Greek beach and, in a diamond shape, on a page torn from an exercise book, my first love poem: "I / am nigh / lovers sigh ... the sweet bare bracken there to lie", and so on. I was under the influence of Dylan Thomas. Our English teacher had played us a record of the prologue to *Under Milk Wood*. I immediately got Thomas's poems out of the library. I remember being sent home from a birthday party for inserting lines from some of the more sexually suggestive ones into a game of consequences.

I studied music at university. My first choice had been medicine but the headmistress decided I wasn't temperamentally suited to be a doctor. I should have read English but "English degrees are two-a-penny" pronounced my mother who had one. I fell in love, got pregnant, married, and produced a baby as I went into my finals year. After graduating, I taught music unenthusiastically in a girls' private school, had three more children, wrote odd lines of poems, felt isolated and unfulfilled.

It wasn't until I moved to London in my mid-thirties, weaned myself off anti-depressants, and wandered into a poetry class with the safeguard that I would "just give it a try", that I began to write seriously.

The tutor, Colin Falck, was a brilliant teacher. Each week we analysed the work of a published poet in the first half of the session, and the work of one of the students in the second, applying the same critical standards to both. Edward Thomas, Tom Paulin, Douglas Dunn (we looked at *Terry Street*) and William Carlos Williams were, at this time, the poets who impressed me most.

Alan Ross published my first poem in *The London Magazine* in 1979. I had gone to the hairdressers to have a frizzy perm to cheer myself up. I needn't have bothered. I found his letter when I got back suggesting some improvements to the poem, which I made. If only all editors were as helpful and encouraging.

It was incredibly important for me: the step to published poet. Living in Newcastle in the late sixties and early seventies, I had known Tony Harrison and his wife (we were in the same baby-sitting circle). He ran a poetry class. If I had joined, it might have started me writing much sooner. But he had once mentioned, with withering scorn, an "unpublished poetess". He knew nothing about my ambitions; but I smarted for days, as if he did.

Almost the first poem I wrote, 'Slow Reader', was about my five-year-old son: "When I take him on my knee / with his Ladybird book ... he gazes into the air / sighing and shaking his head / like an old man who thinks the mountains / are impassable". The poem, I now realise, was as much to do with my fears about venturing onto the slopes of Parnassus as it was about his reluctance to read. At the end, I liken him to

> a white eyed colt,
> shying from the bit, who sees
> that if he takes it in his mouth
> he'll never run quite free again.

Learning to read, the analogy implies, signals the end of a child's abandonment to animal pleasures. It involves loss as well as gain. But becoming a poet also involves the end of a kind of innocence. It is about being critical, separate. Experience is no longer just experience. It becomes material.

My first collection of poems, *Close Relatives*, appeared in 1981. It was not until 1994, thirteen years later, that Cape published *The Handless Maiden*. It is difficult to analyse exactly why. In 1981 I went back to university to take a degree in English and then began a PhD. That certainly arrested my writing for a time; though, in the long term, the exposure to all that literature — even if the poetry consisted almost exclusively of a long line of male poets — had a good effect.

I got round to reading women poets later: Anne Bradstreet, Emily Dickinson, Christina Rossetti, Charlotte Mew, HD, Marianne Moore, Sylvia Plath, Anne Sexton, Elizabeth Bishop, and Elaine Feinstein's translations of the Russian poets Ahkmatova and Tsvetayeva. But their influence was only gradual: a sort of drip-feed of nutrients. It was not until I read Adrienne Rich's essay 'When We Dead Awaken: Writing as Re-Vision' that I properly realised how important this shadow line of women poets was to me; and, also, how resistant I had been to women's voices and visions.

Rich addresses this resistance through an analysis of her own development as a poet. Her earliest models, like mine, were the male poets she had studied at college. She had been taught, as I had, "that poetry should be 'universal' which meant, of course, nonfemale". Even when, in the sequence 'Snapshops of a Daughter-in-Law', she had felt able to write, for the first time, directly about experiencing herself as a woman, she still "hadn't found the courage to use the pronoun 'I' — the woman in the poem is always 'she'". "She" was a device I had used frequently in my first book as a way of making my poems appear less autobiographical. The effect was to split me off from emotions that allowed into the poems might have given them more energy and conviction.

Another problem was form. When I attempted to write quatrains or sonnets, what spark of life there was in my work quickly died. I wrote free-verse; but because of an underlying unease at not using established patterns — the niggly voices saying "You're not a proper poet" — I couldn't allow myself the freedom to let my voice create its own forms. Adrienne Rich's solution was to experiment with trying to create an alternative feminine language. But I didn't find this particularly helpful as a model.

Then I discovered the work of the American poet Sharon Olds. *The Sign of Saturn*, her selected poems, was published in England in 1991. Emily Dickinson compares herself in one poem to a volcano. It is a good image for Olds, too. She writes about sex, children, and family relationships with a molten lyricism that owes nothing to existing forms. I don't think all the poems work. But they matter. They don't just cover the paper. They have a passion in their delivery, a riskiness, a precision and sensuality in the way they describe experience that spurred me to want to invest my poems with a similar honesty and edge.

For two weeks in the summer of 1990 I stayed at Annaghmakerrig, a house in County Monaghan that is run as a centre for artists. There was a lake to swim in, tracks through woods and heathland, a room with a desk and coal fire and, in the evening, communal meals and, at the end of a three-mile walk that on cloudy nights had to be negotiated by the feel of your feet on the road, a bar. But in the daytime there was no one to talk to. On the first day, I wrote in my notebook:

> I remember Charlotte Mew writing once, you can only experience things on your own. But it's so lonely on your own. When I've found hands, I can go back to the world of men.

The finding of hands related to a fairy story that had begun to obsess me. Several years before I'd printed 'THE HANDLESS MAIDEN' in black ink on the brown paper cover of a notebook made in China, that I loved because its thin pages reminded me of the Jeyes toilet paper I had written on as a child. But the pages remained empty. The story of a girl whose hands are cut off, who finds a husband to give her silver hands and who, eventually, after going off into the forest alone with her child, grows back her own hands, had moved me profoundly but I didn't know why. It wasn't until I read Marie von Franz's feminist-psychoanalytic interpretation of the story that I realised it was my story, and the story of many women. As she points out, it is only the women protagonists of fairy tales who lose their hands. Giving up your own life to live through powerful and creative men is a peculiarly female trait. In the Grimm version of the story the woman's hands grow back because she is good for seven years. In the Russian version, which I prefer, they grow back when she plunges her handless arms into a river to save her drowning baby. She can't bear to lose her child, her own work.

The reference to Charlotte Mew was to a letter she had written from Boulogne in 1911:

> It makes all the difference to me to be in the right place. I should never have done 'Fete' if I hadn't been here last year. One realises the place much more alone I think — it is all there is — you don't feel it through another mind which mixes up things — I wonder if art — as they say, is a rather inhuman thing.

That, too, I had held in my head for a long time, as if waiting for this moment. It made all the difference to me to get away from a full-time teaching job, the end of a seven year long love-affair, and a house with a crack to be on my own at Annamaghkerrig.

After several attempts to find a way of writing about The Handless Maiden, I gave up. But the idea of going away on my own to grow back my hands was a powerful incentive to write as well as an antidote to grief. I used the place, specifically the pond in the garden, as the setting for a poem, 'The Lily Pond', which converts the grief — which could so easily have formed the material for an embarrassing confessional poem — into a dramatic soliloquy.

The combination of murder and resurrection in the poem's first two lines —

> Thinking of new ways to kill you
> and bring you back from the dead ...

— originated in a diary entry written before I left England:

> Maybe it's better not to talk to people about — . It always upsets me. I just have to lay him under a sheet in my mind, as if he were dead. And then believe that if by some miracle he wakes, that would be his doing.

Below this there was an attempt to start a poem:

> I lay you under a sheet, as if you were dead.
> Then, I must go away and lead my life —
> not wait at the entrance to the tomb
> so as not to be far away
> if by some miracle you wake.

The image of laying a body under a sheet also survived into the finished poem (see page 154); but the references to "the entrance to the tomb" and "miracle" disappeared. They would have given an unwanted Christian gloss to what I intended more to resemble a pagan ritual.

A couple of weeks later, now at Annaghmakerrig, I wrote in my notebook:

> I ought to go out into the garden in the sun. I mustn't while I'm here feel I have to do anything to please or impress other people. I am here for myself, to write — because that is what I want to do. And it doesn't matter how I go about it. I'm not writing a novel. I'm writing *poems*. And they come about in curious ways. I could read all day; or sleep all day; or walk all day. It only takes 10 minutes to write a poem — or the germ, skeleton of one.

Actually in the garden, and sitting by the pond, what I produced seems particularly unpromising:

> The Pond
> needs clearing/groundsel
> The wound.
> If I am still and listen hard enough ...
> A bee buzzes past
> Seeds drift upwards/ dead
> The dead...
> The wind lifting, ruffling.
> the DREAM. I'm going to write one poem here with that title. I'm going to have an important dream — but it won't just be about the dream — it will contain the actual world and my thoughts about it.

These ramblings were almost all discarded. But I had got myself by the pond, using my senses — "the wind ruffling, lifting" — and making connections between my feelings inside and the world outside. I had also got the idea of a poem that would combine actuality and dream.

The next step was backwards. I went off into metaphor, always my weakness:

Hope

can't be given up —
it wouldn't be hope.
Even if I plunged it
into this pond, held it down
under the matted weed
it would bob up like a cork.

It was not entirely useless because the idea of holding hope down was later transformed, without the bathos of the bobbing cork, into the stronger and more shocking image of holding a head down.

What follows goes back to the sheet, and a new development, which also ended up in the finished poem — climbing in under it too:

I lay them beside you
under a white sheet
as if you were dead
and then climb under the same sheet
in case by some miracle you wake.

At this point I went back to the pond to make more direct observations. For the first time, the title appears:

The Lily Pond
is all clogged up. There's more weed
than water and only two lilies, the wind
rocking them as a dragonfly skims over.
My bum is stiff/numb with sitting
on the stone. In my head I keep
pushing you under, holding you
under the mat of weed —

I need my voice back — where is it?

Gradually, elements of the finished poem — matted weed, the wind rocking the lilies, dragonflies — were beginning to appear. At the time, though, it must have seemed hopeless. I abandoned it and began working on a poem about making an apple tart (never completed).

But somehow 'The Lily Pond' was writing itself in my head. Later
that day, I began the poem again. Pages of my notebook are filled
with drafts. Here is one that bears some resemblance to the finished
poem, though I still haven't got the beginning.

> I drown you in the lily pond,
> holding your head down
> under the flat leaves
> and spiky flowers
> that float over you like a wreath.
>
> Then I sit until I am numb
> watching the wind
> rock the flowers,
> lift the leaves and you rise to the surface.
>
> I could wake [sic] away free.
> But I drag you onto the stones
> and lie close to your cold
> weed-slimed body
> in case by some miracle you wake.

The next draft of the poem which makes a significant change is
on a page torn from a notebook. I can't date it. The first two lines
are almost as in the finished version. The poem has found its form
of three-line stanzas too:

> Trying to think of a new way to kill you
> and bring you to life again
> I drown you in the lily pond,
>
> holding your head down
> until every bubble of breath
> is squeezed from your lungs
>
> and the flat leaves
> and spiky flowers
> float over you like a wreath.
>
> I sit on the stones until I'm numb,
> watching a wind
>
> A breeze rocks the lilies,
> lifts the edges of the leaves,
> blue dragonflies
>
> hover in the air like ghosts

Here the draft ends. I can't find any further drafts. I must have typed them on sheets of paper that got lost or thrown away.

Until I looked back in my notebook, I had sustained the myth in my mind that I sat by the pond one afternoon and wrote the poem almost straight out. In fact, as with nearly all my poems, the process of writing it involved a series of messy, chaotic attempts to reach a bit closer towards a version that finally emerges as more realised and ordered.

> Thinking of new ways to kill you
> and bring you back from the dead,
> I try drowning you in the lily pond —
>
> holding your head down
> until every bubble of breath
> is squeezed from your lungs
>
> and the flat leaves and spiky flowers
> float over you like a wreath.
> I sit on the stones until I'm numb,
>
> until, among reflections of sky,
> water-buttercups, spears of iris,
> your face rises to the surface —
>
> a face that was always puffy
> and pale, so curiously unchanged.
> A wind rocks the waxy flowers, curls
>
> the edges of the leaves. Blue dragonflies
> appear and vanish like ghosts.
> I part the mats of yellow weed
>
> and drag you to the bank, covering
> your green algae-stained corpse
> with a white sheet. Then, I lift the edge
>
> and climb in underneath —
> thumping your chest,
> breathing into your mouth.

When 'Lily Pond' won a prize in a poetry competition in which the poems were entered anonymously, the judges assumed it had been written by a man. This probably reveals more about stereo-typed preconceptions of gender identity (only men write violent poems) than any real divisions between what is male and female in poetry.

I was certainly conscious, after I had written the poem, that I had broken through to a voice that was braver and fiercer than before, though I'd come close to it in an earlier poem 'Woodpigeons', written in revenge after a stressful dinner party.

A few months before I had read Lorca's lecture on *duende* (printed at the back of the Penguin *Selected Poems*) and found exciting the idea of art originating in a power "that has to be roused in the the very cells of blood". I made a conscious decision to try and draw on this energy in my writing. The words "wound" and "death" that appear disconnectedly in the first draft of 'Lily Pond' may be references to Lorca's identification of *duende* with death and suffering: "The *duende* does not appear if it sees no possibility of death ... [It] likes the edge of things, the wound".

But women have also identified with the need for violence and ferocity in their writing. Virginia Woolf felt that she had to "kill" the Angel in the House before she could write uncensored. Sylvia Plath spoke of the "blood jet" of poetry, Emily Dickinson of a "loaded gun", and Stevie Smith, in the most violent images she could muster, of "an explosion in the sky ... a mushroom shape of terror", of the human creature "alone in its carapace" forcing a passage out "in splinters covered with blood". Poetry, she wrote, "never has any kindness at all".

It has been so difficult for women — the soothers and carers and comforters — to be good poets. Every term at my all girls' school we were read the beautiful passage from Proverbs: "The Price of a good woman is above rubies ... She walks behind her husband in the gates ... She clothes her family in scarlet". It entered my consciousness so deeply I bought scarlet flannel to line my children's duffle coats. It was a long time before I found the necessary anger and distance to express my ambivalence at such seductive but potentially imprisoning images.

I managed it finally in a poem called 'Ironing'. Its structure is based on George Herbert's poem 'The Flower'. The conjunction of seventeenth century priest and twentieth century feminist is not as unlikely as it might seem when you think of the angry dialogue with God in his poem 'The Collar' ("I struck the board, and cry'd, No more"). A Freudian might even see an unconscious link in the word "board".

A spiritual autobiography in miniature, Herbert's poem uses the cycle of a flower through winter into spring as a metaphor for the

death and regrowth of the soul. My poem is a mini-autobiography
too: only I take my metaphor not from nature but from my life as a
woman — my relationship with ironing.

> I used to iron everything:
> my iron flying over sheets and towels
> like a sledge chased by wolves over snow,
>
> the flex twisting and crinking
> until the sheath frayed, exposing
> wires like nerves. I stood like a horse
>
> with a smoking hoof
> inviting anyone who dared
> to lie on my silver-padded board,
>
> to be pressed to the thinness
> of dolls cut from paper.
> I'd have commandeered a crane
>
> if I could, got the welders at Jarrow
> to heat me an iron the size of a tug
> to flatten the house.
>
> Then for years I ironed nothing.
> I put the iron in a high cupboard.
> I converted to crumpledness.
>
> And now I iron again: shaking
> dark spots of water onto wrinkled
> silk, nosing into sleeves, round
>
> buttons, breathing the sweet heated smell
> hot metal draws from newly-washed
> cloth, until my blouse dries
>
> to a shining, creaseless blue,
> an airy shape with room to push
> my arms, breasts, lungs, heart into.

Just before I began writing the poem, I had jotted down two notes
about pieces in *The Guardian*. One was by the art critic Tim Hilton
on a Holbein portrait of a woman with a pet squirrel and starling.
"She has such a lovely face — serious, studious," I wrote. Then:

> Tim Hilton says the painting is not symbolic — but I wonder.

> Squirrels and starlings are fierce. The squirrel — woman's
> feelings on a chain. The starling — her squawking voice.

The second was a quotation from Saul Bellow on how Mozart's
music was produced without effort:

> What it makes us see is that there are things which must be
> done easily. Easily or not at all — that is the truth about art.

"If that is true," I added, "I ought to give up trying to be a poet."
In retrospect, both these jottings relate in a significant way to the
poem. They show that I was already thinking about two opposing
aspects of a woman: the lovely calm madonna's face in contrast to
the fierceness of her feelings (symbolised by the squirrel) and jarring
voice (symbolised by the starling).

I was also worrying about the idea that art should come easily.
Keats said it, too, even more categorically: "If poetry comes not as
naturally as leaves to a tree it had better not come at all". Because
I've always have such a battle with poems, his words have stuck in
my mind, internalised as a rebuke that on the one hand makes me
want to give up writing, and on the other to rage against them. After
all, giving birth is natural — and how many babies are born easily?
It is another reason why I was drawn to Lorca. *Duende* celebrates
the idea that art involves a struggle.

One way I defeat the critical voices that tell me to give up even
before I've started is to keep a notebook. I fill it with shopping lists,
student marks, quotations, fragments of a diary, resolutions to lead
a more organised life, and, before I commit myself to the terror and
potential failure of actually writing a poem, with "notes" for poems.
This is the page headed 'IRONING (notes for)':

> Soothing/smoothing/smell/steam
> Weight of my hand & arm & shoulder
> push into sleeve, the crumpled fabric,
> a blouse, silk, purple, violet, crumpled
> smooth   heat/dampness, the smell of
> washed clothes which I know is synthetic
> but I am deceived by its smell to believe its natural,
> like in a bluebell wood
> (Look Back in Anger/Dashing Away with a Smoothing Iron —
> I used to sing with my father — he stole my heart away.)
> For the years of my children's childhood
> I ironed everything (the good mother) even for six months
> starch tea-towels (tv ad for spray on starch).

Then for years I ironed nothing.
'Your clothes always look as if they've just come out of
the laundry basket,' a woman whose husband fancied me
told me.
The iron itself — like a mechanical mouse with a long tail.

Only the seeds of the finished poem are in this first draft: but
among them is the antithesis that provides the poem's argument —
"For years ... I ironed everything" and, the only line to have survived
intact, "Then for years I ironed nothing".

Various elements have been disposed of altogether. "The good
mother" I must have rejected because it was too obvious and
because I was more interested in the revolt against domesticity. The
synthetic bluebell smell of the detergent was too banal, a distraction
from the central idea of the poem. The song I sang with my father,
'Dashing Away With a Smoothing Iron', went too. The emotion
was too soft for what I wanted. The anecdote about the woman who
said my clothes looked as if they had come out of a laundry basket
must have seemed too exposing and confessional. The idea stays
with "I converted to crumpledness".

The anger in the finished poem is fairly muted in the first draft,
expressed only in the title of John Osborne's *Look Back in Anger* —
a play which, of course, begins with a woman ironing while the men
sit and read the Sunday papers. It is certainly not in the simile of
the iron as a mouse.

I don't usually go in consciously for "Martian-style" similes. But
I wanted to make the iron a real physical presence in the poem; to
create a series of dream-like and slightly menacing pictures, rather
like Paula Rego's nursery-rhyme illustrations. But I rejected the
mouse, for its associations with timidity. I replaced it with a whole
string of visual similes — a "sledge chased by wolves over snow",
"wires like nerves" and a "smoking hoof" — that are not only closer
graphically to an iron but that also reflect more effectively the stress
and anger of the narrator's emotions. The further images of paper
dolls and an "iron the size of a tug" were added both for their
emotional weight and because they came from my life at the time.
Like lots of mothers I helped my children cut strings of skirted and
trousered figures out of folded paper. Living in Newcastle, I had
visited Jarrow to see a ship being launched.

The "notes" for the poem were actually written after ironing a
blouse. Though greatly worked on, the sensual details of colour and
smell have remained, moved from the opening of the poem to the
end in the interests of the argument. This section of the finished

poem, beginning "And now I iron again ...", draws directly on
Herbert's

> And now in age I bud again
> After so many deaths I live and write;
> I once more smell the dew and rain
> and relish versing.

Ever since I first read them, these lines have affected me powerfully. It is partly because of the subject — the possibility of new life
and renewal after what I imagine as a series of depressions. But it is
also because they break out of the poem's controlling metaphysical
metaphor — the flower — into describing, simply and directly,
Herbert's own pleasure in sensual experience: in dew and rain and
writing.

I wanted my poem to do something similar: to mark the emotional
journey from ironing as a metaphor for the constriction of domestic
life to ironing as a celebration of domesticity — of its sensual
pleasures and, when there's a choice, its freedoms.

My aim in *The Handless Maiden* was to bring together poems that
came from my own experience, such as 'Lily Pond' and 'Ironing',
with poems that drew on myths, fairy stories, and sometimes
paintings, that reflected or illumined or reinforced it. In the poem
'Judith', for example, based on the bible story, I found it easy,
because of my own feelings of grief and anger and longing, to enter
the mind of a woman who used her grief and rage to cut off the head
of Holofernes.

The title poem was finally written in a month's stay at Hawthornden Castle, a retreat for writers near Edinburgh. The castle is
perched on a sandstone cliff and the "brimming river" with banks
of "red-orange mud" that appears in the poem was the torrent,
swollen with rain (it was April), that ran in the gorge below. "I think
again of writing The Handless Maiden — it's so important to me;
if the poem was good enough it could be the title of the book", I
decided on the first night. And significantly, because the idea that
I am the handless maiden, writing my story with my new-grown
hands, is what finally gave the poem its final image and meaning, I
also wrote:

> I haven't brought any typing paper. I'll have to get some. But
> I want to wait a week until next Tuesday. Just keep writing
> until then. The typewriter is a distraction. I want poems to
> come out of my own hand, my body. That connects to The

Handless Maiden — last line of poem? these words — / with
my own hands / I write them [sic].

There were numerous false-starts. For example:

This is my hand
holding the pen
that scratches the paper.

And another:

I cut off my own hands.
One for my mother. One for my father.
If they couldn't be mine
no one would own them.

Worse:

I cut off my hands:
saw them lying on the grass,
bloody, like two fish.

And:

Alone in the world
I tied my shoelaces
with tongue and teeth.

Ten days later I was getting desperate:

Maybe I ought to try writing haiku. NO! NO! NO! You must
go on trying to get your own voice back; it will come; it's
come before.

Then, after pages and pages of more false-starts, I wrote:

Vicki, stop! You're getting nowhere: it's just a metaphor —
not important; or perhaps it is — but the only way of writing
the story would be to get into it; to have a real sense of losing
your hands and growing them. Read the story again — maybe
it's in the library — and just deal with that moment when she
dips her arms into the water and her hands start to grow!

From that moment on I knew how to write the poem: by putting
myself into the woman at the moment when she rescues her baby,
when her hands grow. But I was still a long way from the finished

version. On the next page there's a draft that fumbles towards it:

> I plunged my handless arms
> into the stream, the stream running
> deep and cloudy with all the earth
> the rain has washed from the banks
> I couldn't see my baby; I ... [illegible]
> into the water, I ...[illegible]
> and then I touched her curled hand
> with the smooth skin of my stump
> and couldn't grasp it and ... [illegible]
> out of my wrist bones, to grow
> and muscle and skin and strong
> fingers, and felt a tingling and a pain
> like the pain of giving birth
> and I grasped her fingers, pulled her
> out of the water, spluttering, the water
> running out of her mouth, and when
> I'd laid on the grass,
> and dried her
> and she was breathing, and gurgling
> I looked at the miracle
> of my hands and thought I'd cut them off
> because if I didn't own them nobody would,
> and of the silver hands my husband gave me,
> how they were useless, except to do
> what he wanted, and that all the time
> my hands would have grown
> if I'd reach out for what I wanted
> what I couldn't bear to lose.

The essential elements of the poem are in this draft. But it still took pages and pages of editing before it arrived at its final shape. I went through alternate periods of despair ("I'm struggling and getting nowhere with 'The Handless Maiden'. It would be better to give up") and of renewed attempts to find a way to make the poem work ("I have to stay inside the story but empower it with my feelings").

Here is a late draft that it is interesting to compare with the finished poem:

> When all the water had run from her mouth
> and I'd rubbed her arms and legs
> and chest and belly and back
> with grass, and felt her heat
> passing into my breast

and shoulder, and the breath
I couldn't believe in
like a tickling feather
on my neck, I cried.
I cried for the hands
that the devil made my father cut off
I cried for the beautiful silver hands
my husband, the king, gave me
that spun and wove and embroidered
but had no feeling.
I cried for the itching,
lumpy scar-tissue of my stumps.
And I cried for the hands
that write this — strong,
long-boned hands, flowering
in the river's cloudy
red-orange flood,
grasping my baby's curled fists.

The opening lines are there. The poem has found its final narrative shape. But some significant differences exist between this and the finished poem. There were some excisions. I took out "the devil". It belonged to the world of the fairy story and seemed only to confuse my simplified and condensed and, hopefully, more realistic version. For the same reason I took out "the king". I also removed, with some reluctance — I love the sound of the word and the image it conjures — "and embroidered" from the description of the silver hands.

The main changes are additions. I wanted to delay the litany of "I cried" for as long as possible, so I extended the poem's opening narrative by imagining what I would have done if I had just rescued my baby from drowning. I changed "grass" to "clumps of dried moss", a detail that like the "red-orange flood" (changed to "mud" in the final version) came out of walking along the river bank at Hawthornden. And I added other practical details — putting the baby "to sleep in a nest of grass" and spreading "her dripping clothes on a bush" — to make the narrative more down-to-earth and believable.

The principal addition to the second part of the poem is to include the moment when the baby falls into the river. I wanted it there to make the rescue seem even more miraculous. In the final version, before "And I cried for my hands" ("the" is changed to "my" to make it more emphatic, more personal), I inserted an account of the baby

unwinding
from the tight swaddling cloth
as I drank from the brimming river.

There is no swaddling cloth in the original story. I borrowed it from
Nativity plays to re-enact with its "unwinding" the sensation of
slow-motion, of inevitability, as something terrible happens.

   Finally, the ending was tightened; the language made tougher.
"Flowered" was changed to "sprouted". "The river's cloudy /
red-orange flood" became, more economically, "the red-orange
mud". The adjectives "strong, long-boned" disappeared: they in-
terfered with the main point of the hands — that they are "the hands
that write this". I wanted the poem to move seamlessly from
beginning to end: the essence of the story, of what it meant to me,
captured in a single impassioned speech.

> When all the water had run from her mouth,
> and I'd rubbed her arms and legs,
> and chest and belly and back,
> with clumps of dried moss;
> and I'd put her to sleep in a nest of grass,
> and spread her dripping clothes on a bush,
> and held her again — her heat passing
> into my breast and shoulder,
> the breath I couldn't believe in
> like a tickling feather on my neck,
> I let myself cry. I cried for my hands
> my father cut off; for the lumpy, itching scars
> of my stumps; for the silver hands
> my husband gave me — that spun and wove
> but had no feeling; and for my handless arms
> that let my baby drop — unwinding
> from the tight swaddling cloth
> as I drank from the brimming river.
> And I cried for my hands that sprouted
> in the red-orange mud — the hands
> that write this, grasping
> her curled fists.

"The hands that write this" are, as I have implied, my hands. But
the story is, for me, both true and not true. For long periods I am
again handless. I have to go on repeating it. The writing of each
poem involves a journey into a "forest" of drafts and because, in a
sense, the poem already exists, the plunging of handless arms into
a river to recover what "I couldn't bear to lose".

Don Paterson
The Dilemma of the Peot

> The reader may be witness to the miracle but may never
> participate in it; poetry must remain a private transaction
> between the author and God. The true poem is no more than
> a spiritual courtesy, the act of returning a borrowed book.
>
> François Aussemain, *Pensées*

My Dad found a wee school jotter of mine the other week in the loft; it must've been written when I was six or so, one of those story-and-picture jobs we were obliged to write up every morning. One entry, dated December '69, reads: "when I grow up i am giong to be a peot, and rite peoms". Apart from this isolated flash of prescience, the next fifteen years went by without the idea occurring to me again. The prediction wasn't strictly accurate: I now write peoms, but I'll never feel like I'm a peot. Poetry, like murder, describes an act, not necessarily a permanent disposition, and it's the act of poetry I'll be trying to describe here, not the condition of being a practitioner, which is quite illusory — and always something of a retrospective aggrandisement. A poet should be in service to the poem, and while that's the case, nothing exists except the poem; the poem annihilates the poet. I might feel like a poet after the poems are written, but since I'm no longer writing them, I can't be; it's just self-congratulation.

A great hero of mine, the American critic Randall Jarrell, said that a poem is a way of forgetting how you came to write it; if that's true, and I think it probably is, all of what follows is complete lies, a little *post hoc* indulgence. Furthermore, to air a familiar cliché, the creative process for most writers is deeply mysterious, and some attempt has to be made to preserve that mystery, so it'd hardly be in my own interests to tell you very much ... I remember some geezer at a literary conference — he was representing some unreadable wee critical theory magazine — complaining that, although the work itself exhibited considerable intelligence, there was far too little intelligent discussion by the poets themselves of the poetic process. The reply to that is very simple; a lot of writers preserve the mystery by keeping it at a pre- or sub-linguistic level. When poets get together — as they often do — it's the last thing, in my experience, they ever discuss. I'd, if I were you, be deeply suspicious of any poet who claims to understand, and who will cheerfully expatiate on the "process". Poetry, for me at least, is still an occult science (we shouldn't forget that Gilles de Rais, the original Bluebeard, was charged — along with murder, alchemy, necromancy and unnatural sexual intercourse — with the crime of *poetry*) and a form of shamanism: and you can always tell a fake shaman, because they're too keen to divulge their trade secrets in order to impress you. (Stand up, Kenneth White.) I'm keen to impress you too, but if I told you my tricks they wouldn't work anymore, assuming any of them work in the first place. Like any occult practitioner, there are several heresies to which the poet must consciously or unconsciously subscribe — it would take a book to talk about them all, and even then, I wouldn't — but the main one, for me at least, is that *word and object are the same thing.* Poetry differs from prose in that it has less to do with its subject matter, and is principally *a form of address*: the manner in, and the degree of obliquity with which the subject is broached. It's also a matter of trajectory — prose is horizontal, an evocative discipline, the business of describing things so vividly it's as if one were actually present; poetry is vertical, invocatory, where things are called down from above by the mere intonation of their names; for me, there's no "as if" in poetry. In the beginning was the word, not the world, and poetry reminds us of this continually.

I don't have any formulae for writing poems. Trying to write another good poem by recreating the circumstances and repeating the techniques that allowed you to write the last one is as daft as making love in the same situation, at the same time and in the same position, in the hope that you might recreate a child with the same physique and personality as the last. The almost infinitely long concatenation of causally related events whereby children and poems come into being is real enough, but far too complex for us to understand. Any systematic explanation would be quite worthless, so I'm not going to attempt one, just set down a few things that are important to me. Some, I think, are generally applicable; others are probably too personal and idiosyncratic to be of any use to anyone, though they may be of some voyeuristic interest.

I remember Michael Longley saying that poems needed a sperm and ovum, a male and female component to exist; two things come together — a familiar situation or utterance that is suddenly seen in a different context, even just two words that you'd hadn't though of putting together before, from which the poem develops organically. Almost invariably, poems arrive in the form of words, not ideas. I don't think poets get ideas for poems, they get words; that's their gift, and they forget it at their peril. Punters get ideas for poems, your Dad and your mates do, and are always suggesting suitable topics. To embroider Longley's analogy: the act of composition is a love affair, and the poem itself the offspring. Like all love affairs, the poem should surprise or scare the shit out of you, and allows you to reinvent yourself, or discover a part of yourself you knew nothing of. (Actually, in a Buddhistic sense, the poem teaches you that you're no more than an infinitely malleable, reprogrammable set of habits and characteristics: nothing, in other words.) And like all love affairs, your relationship with the poem is completely obsessive.

There's this idea, explicit in Buddhist teaching but which you can infer in Borges, Calvino, Jung, Derrida and a thousand other writers, that God dispersed after the Big Bang, or after the Fall, and shattered into a million pieces, like a great glass hologram. The pieces are us. A poem is the literary analogue, a highly polished shard of the Great Epic: "there is one story and one story only," as Graves said, and the whole is subtly implied in the fragmentary narratives that we write. (Every shard of a laser hologram, contains, amazingly, the whole picture.) As a perfect analogue, so it's also a perfect mirror, and depending on how we turn these shards, how we allow the light to catch them, we can see something of our true nature in them. Now I'm sorry if I'm coming over like a terrible hippy, but I'm absolutely scunnered with writers who refuse to acknowledge the spiritual dimension in their work. I'm not going to sit here telling you that for me poetry is like any other job, like carpentry or rug-making. It isn't. There's the craft and the graft, sure, but there's a whole lot more besides. The whole lot more, alas, is mostly beyond the scope of this essay, but I'll tell you as much as I know about the other stuff.

So what usually happens is that I get this wee phrase in my head that I can't leave alone; sometimes it's original, sometimes a cliché or some bit of received language I've discovered something new in; it constantly surprises me when I think about it, and that's completely essential — if it doesn't surprise me, I can't expect it to surprise the reader, which is the whole point of the exercise: to blow the reader's mind. I can't stop thinking about it, and it soon develops into a full-blown obsession. At this stage I've absolutely no idea where it's leading me — which is another reason I think "subject matter" such an irrelevancy — but I can feel the energy of it, and have learned to trust that and go with it. I tend not to write things down in notebooks till a little later ... it's true that "ideas don't keep appointments", but if the words can't live in the synapses for a little while they probably don't deserve to be written down, any more than you should have to remind yourself who it is that you're in love with. So this first stage is a matter of learning to distinguish between what's a poem and what isn't. I've even learned, should I get what I think of as a great *idea* for a poem when walking down the street, to discount it immediately, because it's arrived in the wrong form — one which flatters my own intelligence, one which bolsters my ego, not dissolves it. I've also had to learn to leave a lot of poems where I found them, since they're already complete — all those sunsets and rainbows and cathedrals ... we should remember that the poet's job is to make the commonplace miraculous (actually the greater responsibility is to make the commonplace commonplace, the present the present, "the stone stony" — to render the world back to the world — but that's an evolutionary stage quite beyond me in this life) and commonplace miracles like sunsets and rainbows and cathedrals leave us, usually, with very little we can constructively add. So I've had to learn to distinguish between the poetic *feeling* that comes over us — which everyone experiences — and the true poetic urge, the urge to *make* a poem, which only poets do. We only steal these "life-poems" from ourselves anyway, that we might bask in a little of the reflected glory. A true poem has to be made up, not stolen. (Invariably when we try to steal them they backfire, because a poem is often a motif or event set in an harmonically unique context; and in life, that's too complex, or too perfect, to ever fully recreate.) Remember that story of Bosko and Admira, the Serbian and Moslem lovers that were found shot dead in one another's arms on that bridge in Sarajevo? You could sense immediately that it was going to spawn a billion lousy poems. It was a beautiful story, heartbreaking, and what too many people failed to realise — unimprovable. Changing that one iota is no less presumptuous than adding or subtracting a line from a Basho haiku.

Anyway, the bit after that initial germination is quite strange (I'm going to mix these metaphors of childbirth and love affairs quite freely, so forgive me); things still progress in an organic way, without me feeling that I'm doing much work ... Again, if there isn't a spell where I feel like I'm writing effortlessly, even for a few lines, I suspect the poem of being willed into existence, rather than choosing me to bring it to life; I think true poems choose you just as children are said to choose their parents. I've had my fair share of phantom pregnancies, though, but I'm getting better at spotting them early. If there isn't an element of the poem that's "given", even a few lines or so, I don't trust it. So at this stage there's a lot of what you might call verification, checking that what I'm working on is really a poem, and that I'm not going to waste a whole month on a complete turkey like I did last time. So I go away and do something else, shoot pool, play music, catch a movie, write a review, then come back and open the notebook and look at what I've written. If it's going to be a poem — and this is crucial — *I don't immediately understand* what I've written. I don't understand it because it isn't telling me something I knew already. I know it's come from somewhere else, so I get scared; as André Previn once remarked: if you do good work you should be scared by it. Then I get the shivers, or I burst into tears, or I get totally blissed out. Man. At this point I'm always reminded of Borges's brilliant definition of the aesthetic fact: *the imminence of a revelation which does not come.* You should feel like God's in the next room — nearly, but not quite, deigning to grant you an audience. Anything much less than that and I'm probably doing nothing more than bringing another mediocre poem into the world, and there's far too much useless junk floating round the universe already. Whether my poem is brilliant or not is neither here nor there — what's important is that *I'm* convinced it is.

Time for a quick word about ... stationery. Most poets are fetishistic about paper and pens, and at the moment I can't write on anything but grey Daler A5 sketchbooks with a Pilot Hi-Tecpoint V5 extra-fine rollerball. OK? It's taken me a pathetically long time to realise that the transcendental joy of poetry isn't getting your book published, reading to an audience of deeply-moved young women, getting your face on the box, winning a prize or anything else — it's the business of composition that blows you away, and the more you can do to savour it, the better. I think it's important to pay attention to those little ritualistic details which serve to put you in a receptive state of mind — even just the purchase of stationery is enough to do that for me, pathetic as it may seem. I often go to cafés to write; in fact the greater the extraneous racket the better I can often concentrate. Even McDonald's suits me just great. My current favourite, though, is the tower café at Dundee University, which as well as the racket, has a breathtaking view over the Firth of Tay, if I need to feel a bit Parnassian. Libraries are bloody useless, far too quiet, no view, and no way of getting a cup of coffee.

Where was I. Oh aye. After that, the "inspired" bit, it's my job to try and allow the poem to find its final form; just as often you have this vague sense of inevitability in the first lines of a good song, in those "given" lines you should have the DNA from which the whole poem can be developed, in terms of both its form and content. My

poems are often no more than one long extended metaphor grown
from that one germinated spore on the petri dish, though hopefully
I've concealed that. I also try to keep the poem as short as possible,
for two reasons: firstly, if you choose a form that's slightly too short
for the material you've collated, it acts as a kind of automatic filter
for any stuff you're attached to for sentimental, or more often
egotistical reasons (i.e. stuff that shows *you* off, rather than the
poem), but which has no structural place in the poem — in a first
draft, there's always, always, always some stuff like this ... if I've got
twenty lines-worth of good material, I see if it can be a sonnet, or
four quatrains or whatever. This can lead to very costive syntax if
I'm not prepared to strike a compromise between style and content,
as both require space, and are not always precisely coterminous,
though they should be. The other reason is simply that concision is
a courtesy to the reader, who, you should remember, always has a
thousand better things to do than read your poem.

Ideally, there should be no qualitative difference between the stuff
that's given and the stuff I have to make up — part of the craft is
knowing where to look; poetry's just a condition of being pathologically
sensitive to the weight and texture of words, and that includes words
in the dictionary, the thesaurus and the rhyming dictionary too, all
of which are handy if I get stuck — though usually I find they
eliminate rather than suggest alternatives, which is still pretty useful.

A few weeks later, after the first flush of love has faded, it all starts
to get very humdrum and domestic. All I'm thinking about now are
things like syntax, meter, stanzaic definition and the rhyme scheme,
and the musical consistency of the particular rhetorical idiom the
poem appears to be emerging in. The discoveries and surprises, if
there are any left to be made, are of a lower order; they happen at a
very local, word-for word level, and no longer feel like a win on the
pools, or a glimpse of Elijah's chariot, but are more the sort of
pleasant, serendipitous frisson you get from three cherries on the
fruit machine, or the welcome light of an approaching taxi at three
in the morning. Occasionally, though, the poem can still surprise
you, and it's like discovering, after three years of cohabitation, that
your partner can play the spoons or get both their ankles behind
their head, though that's rarely enough to save the relationship.
Once in a blue moon, it turns out that for the past three months
you've been living with an axe murderer or something, which is
pretty exciting, and the whole poem changes course. Usually,
though, towards the end, me and the poem are scrapping over the
trolley in Sainsbury's about whether to get white or pink bog roll,

we haven't slept together for a month, and I know that pretty soon it'll be time for us to go our separate ways.

From the punter's point of view, the poetry reading usually isn't more than a glorified sales pitch for the book, and is often somewhat less; but for the poet, it can be a way of keeping in touch with those old lovers; sometimes it's very poignant, sometimes pretty awful and embarrassing ... Geez, what did I ever see in her? A nicer sensation is geez, what did she ever see in me? Those ones you want to write all over again, it was so good ... and sometimes, alas, that's exactly what you do.

Which brings me to something else. I'm terrified of repeating myself, and have evolved various strategies to try and counter this — well one, really: keep altering the strategy. The great danger, for me, is to continue to mine a seam long after it's yielded up the last diamond ... after a while, you're not even bringing up coal anymore, just dirt ... but now there's a tiny village near the pithead, with a grocer's and a sub-post office, and it's twinned with some crap sonnet sequence in Normandy; and as laird of the estate, you're often the last person to admit it's no longer a viable concern. Tony Harrison's "Continuous" poems — a series of elegies written after the death of his parents — is a good example of the sort of thing I mean, a wonderful piece of work, but something he should have known when to stop writing; eventually he's just bringing up sediment, sentiment, panning it for the very slightest of conceits, until all he can really tell you is that he's crying on the page again. So I've evolved this rather daft solution, which obviously has its own hazards; I'll try and mine tin one week, uranium the next, jade the week after, and so on ... I'd hate to think I was writing the same poem twice. I like the idea of the poem as a self-contained universe, the national anthem of a wee vernacular Atlantis whose laws, customs, geography and weather could all be derived from its close study ... that's absurd and impossible, of course, but probably not a bad thing to aim for.

Part of the advantage of working formally is that you can think of forms as traps, and devise forms to ensnare the particular beast you're after; obviously you're going to catch something quite different depending on whether you set out with a pea-shooter, an elephant-gun, a mist-net or a lobster pot. There's a problem here, which is that it might seem to legislate against the development of the "individual voice", which in part depends upon the *repetition* of strategies, but that's not something I can be bothered with; if it happens, fine. I believe in poems, though, not poets, so sod the individual voice. All true poems are fugitive, anyway. They're too good for their authors.

If the poem doesn't strike me with the force of a miracle, I assume there's no chance of it striking the reader in that way either; this makes me automatically suspicious of anything that comes too easily. On the other hand it's essential that it should *look* easy, as the best technique obliterates the reader's awareness of *your* technique; I don't want the reader ever to be aware of the meter or the rhyme scheme — these are just the means whereby the spell is woven, if you like. It doesn't make any difference to the patient whether or not they know the chemical constituents of their cough-bottle: that's a matter for the chemist. Yeats is supposed to have been asked why he read so ponderously, pausing at the end of every line. "So they can hear the work I've put in", was his (altogether silly) reply. I don't want anyone to know how much work I've put in. It's a disgrace how much work I've put in. I want everyone to think that God talked to me and I just scribbled it down. Miracles are by definition uncontrived; a contrived miracle is just legerdemain, Paul Daniels, and no one believes in that stuff. Part of the problem, in my case, is that if it looks like it might come too easily, I, or the little Calvinist in me, is in the habit of instituting a some absurdly difficult rhyme scheme or meter to slow me down, especially if the subject matter is guilt-inducing; there's a poem in *Nil Nil* called 'Mooncalf', which no doubt sounds like a bit of gratuitous horror, but came to me in one unbroken, horrendous vision on a tennis court in Brighton ... this woman masturbating and giving birth to a dog ... ugh, I don't want to tell you any more ... Anyway, when I wrote it down, I simply couldn't live with it or myself, so I recast it in four nine-line pentameter stanzas with the daftest rhyme scheme I could devise. Somehow the sheer labour and grief of trying to get it to sound natural had the effect of making me feel less guilty about the subject. I've a couple of wee ballads (rhymed not aBcB, but ABAB, which is a bitch) and rhymed dimeter quatrains (an even bigger bitch) in the new book, written for much the same reason. (I also find that subconscious can operate a lot more freely if I throw the left side of my brain some indigestible intellectual doggy-chew to shut it up and prevent it from interrupting. In that sense, form is like the honey-cake you throw to Cerberus to placate him while you nip into Hades to steal Eurydice back again — and yes, you always turn round before the end, partly so that the revelation can never really take place, partly so you'll have the pleasure of doing it all again some other time. Anyway, the muse cannot, by definition, be successfully wooed in this life. More on this later.) The end result, anyway, is that it takes me forever to finish anything satisfactorily. The one advantage of working so slowly is that I rarely feel completely blocked, since I've always got something half-finished, and by this time stone-cold and completely intractable, to work on that I started three years ago.

Often I find missing words (especially when they've been missing for weeks — I tend to just fill in the stress pattern in the hope that they'll turn up) by constructing them on purely musical criteria. I tend to look at the vowels or the consonantal pattern on either side of the missing word, and just make up some words using the same sounds. If none of them happen to be in English, then I'll look at the nearest words that *do* exist ... Nine times out of ten, I find the solution this way ... it sounds bonkers, I know. I work as a musician, and was a musician long before I wrote poetry; in music there's no ideological conflict between either form and expression (which is why I've never understood people who complain that they find the sonnet form, say, an unbearable restriction, or refer to the "strait-jacket" of the pentameter line) or sound and meaning; they mean precisely the same thing — so whereas to someone else it might seem like an absurd leap of faith, for me it's a fairly natural approach.

This area — the way music and poetry are blurred in my imagination, if not in practice — is probably a bit too obscure and personal to be of much interest to anyone, but I'll mention just one other thing. I'm a big fan of a American pianist called Ritchie Bierach, and I've used a lot of his shorter compositions as structural models for my own shorter poems. There's never one single note in his tunes that isn't advancing the argument in some way; even though you could always say that some of them were structurally unnecessary, the embroidery itself always has some dynamic component, some element of forward motion; and his stuff is full of the most surprising modulations, yet the tune always somehow gets itself back into the original key in the most ingenious and breath-taking fashion — a little circular journey that you didn't know was circular until you turned the very last corner. You can't work out how the hell you got there, yet there's a terrible inevitability to the whole thing ... Within all this, there's this glacial, mathematical internal balance, perfect homoeostasis, a complete evenness of surface tension, nothing so flashy that it detracts from the rest of the tune. Seamus Heaney's work is the nearest thing, for me, in poetry.

I'm obsessive about drafting, and it's almost become a super-stitious thing with me; in the last twenty or thirty drafts of a poem (fifty is about average, I guess, but it varies between ten and eighty, depending on the complexity of the poem, as well as the sheer luck factor) I doubt if anyone else could tell what was changing from page to page; sometimes nothing does, and I'm only writing it out again to get a sense of the thing as a whole, as if I were trying to reduce it to an equation — so I can tell precisely what's not adding up, precisely where the energy is leaking away. My writing is utterly illegible by this point, as I've more or less got the thing off by heart. By this time it's almost an alchemical process, a largely superstitious belief that somehow, by following the same procedure over and over with only tiny modifications from draft to draft, the miracle transformation will take place. The pace is almost evolutionary by this time, which means that the timescale is usually around four to eight months, although the poem might look ninety-five percent complete after a few weeks. For this reason I always have half-a-dozen things on the go at the same time, otherwise I'd never get anything written at all. It always seems, though, that there's always a bit missing at the end, a bit I have to "make up", a bit I'm never happy with ... as if it were part of the contract. What are those lines of Derek Mahon's? "The bump of clay in the Navajo rug put there to mitigate the too godlike perfection of that merely human artefact ..." Ha ha ha.

If there can't, by definition, be a formula for writing good poems, then in a way you're always cheating the system, since the only system that exists is the one that conspires *not* to allow you to write any poems ... and because your brain gets immune very quickly to any new imaginative virus, you can't use the same one twice. You know from experience that certain situations are more likely to generate poems than others; this usually means unsuitable affairs, or the deaths of relatives, both of which you're safer trying to imagine than engineer. One can usually resist the latter, but the former, as it doesn't usually result in prosecution, is, alas, easier to sell to yourself. But other than directly screwing up your life so as to screw a poem out of it, the strategies are usually technical (other people set themselves sestinas and villanelles, or subjects to write about — this never works for me), though there are also various forms of psychological trickery you can employ. One trick is to tell myself, in all earnestness, that I'm embarking on The Great Work, or The Book, as Mallarmé would refer to it: a massive sonnet cycle, 144 interlinked stanzas on the theme of the wild flowers of Forfarshire as a metaphor for the progress of the soul in purgatory, you know the sort of thing. In that way I can sometimes dupe the poetic dynamo, or mangle, in my case, into executing a couple of revolutions before it realises it's not plugged in. It's like going to see the bank manager about a million pound overdraft, and when he refuses, touching him for a tenner which he gives you either out of sheer sympathy, or just to get you out of the place. So you might not have The Book, but you do have a squitty little poem that you didn't have before. But conceal your glee, it might not work the next time.

I think one often writes sustained by necessary myths. With boys it's usually fairly straightforward, and usually involves dangling the tripartite carrot of money, sex and fame (all of which expectations in poetry, are, er ... highly relative concepts, and are, I suspect, steadily eroded in precisely that chronological order) from the end of your pencil: very atavistic urges, primarily concerned with the propagation of the genes, which have their origins in a tingling in the scrotum or the wallet. It's slightly different for girls, as they have a different part of the biological contract, and thus a different set of archetypes — ach, it'd be fun to go into this, but there isn't the space. The poem comes from a higher, and quite ungendered source, but as men we often need a real, not a spiritual carrot to get the thing written. But while it's fine for the ego to *drive* you to the gig, God help you if it's the ego that's up on stage. The main thing is that the poem gets written, so whatever rubbish you have to palm yourself off with is neither here nor there ... provided it doesn't feed back into the poem. I think a degree of self-dramatisation is essential in poetry, a necessary operatic device; but self-aggrandisement is quite different. Bad critics can never tell them apart, but you should.

Of course the most pervasive myth of the lot is that of the Muse; we'd all like God to speak to us directly, but if He did we'd explode, so some form of anthropomorphised mediation is absolutely essential if you're not going to go crazy. It's up to the individual whether this archetype is projected onto a real individual or a blank screen. Muses can be dead, alive or made up. There are several prerequisites: firstly, the muse has to be dumb, all fecundity and prelinguistic chaos, the silent wellspring ... if all this sounds horribly sexist, of course it is: but Beatrice does and always did have her own agenda. We usually don't hear from her, though, either because we've conveniently banged her up in heaven somewhere, or — if she's not dead or made up — because her social milieu tends, conveniently, not to intersect with that of the poet's. Secondly, she should remain resolutely unimpressed by whatever you do, otherwise you'll have little motivation for trying to do it again. This is usually very easy to achieve. Just pick someone who hates poetry.

Even better, just pick someone who hates you. Lastly the relationship — if she's real, and especially if she's dead — should remain
unconsummated, because that infinite delay and anticipation is
precisely what provides the ache, the wound, that hollow feeling that
only art can fill ... temporarily, of course. There are only ever love
poems, really. And if you think that I'm now going to flesh out the
above two paragraphs with some juicy personal anecdotes, you are
sadly deluded.

Poems are translations from the silence, as Charles Simic has
remarked. For me, poems try to put into words that which can't be
put into words ... they're crap, unreliable versions of the songs the
good angels and the bad angels sing, which we're not permitted to
hear ... but sometimes we're standing where we shouldn't be, or
they're standing where they shouldn't be, and we catch a bit of a
refrain, or a single note (which happened to me once; I really heard
it, and can still hear it: Radka Toneff, circa '85, and the girl was
dead soon after for her hubris — okay, so don't believe me) and if
we do we can't help but try to imitate them, the way some birds
can't help but imitate us. So we make these little broken songs, and
they're nearly always sad, because they're broken.

Candlebird*

(after Abbas Ibn Al-Ahnaf, c.750)

If, tonight, she scorns me for my song
You may be sure of this: within the year
Another man will say this verse to her
And she will yield to him for its sad sweetness.

"*Then I am like the candlebird*", he'll continue,
After explaining what a candlebird is,
"*Whose lifeless eyes see nothing and see all,*
Lighting their small room with my burning tongue;

His shadow rears above hers on the wall
As hour by hour, I pass into the air.'
Take my hand. Now tell me: flesh or tallow?
Which I am tonight, I leave to you."

So take my hand and tell me, flesh or tallow.
Which man I am tonight I leave to you.

* Generic name for several species of seabird, the flesh of which
is so saturated in oil the whole bird can be threaded with a wick and
burnt entire

(ABBAS IBN AL-AHNAF)

You've never really suffered, or known
    The anguish of insomnia.
It is I who can never sleep,
    And while I live, I cannot stop
The tears welling out of my eyes.

You scorn me when I speak to you,
    Yet lovers who quote my verse succeed!
I've become a candle thread destined
    To light a room for other men
While burning away into thin air.

36

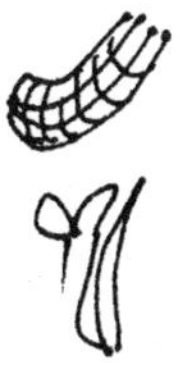

Collected

× If, Knight, she scorns me for my song
× you may be sung of this; within this year,
× another man will sing this same to her
× and she will yield to him for its soft sweetness.

× "When I — like the nightingale", he'll continue,
× this ... explained time — nightingale is
× those ... eyes see ... to see all,
× light ... there still room ... my blazing ...;
× his ... vogue ... the will
× as ... by him, I ... the air.
× I ... my hand, this ... ; first ... fellow?
× Which I — Knight, I ... to you."

× So. Then my hand, the will ... , first ... fellow.
× Which I — Knight I ... to you.

Notes on Contributors

Dannie Abse's most recent book of poems is *On The Evening Road* (Hutchinson). Penguin have published his *Selected Poems* and Seren his *Intermittent Journals*. He is a Fellow of the Royal Society of Literature and President of the Welsh Academy.

Simon Armitage was born in West Yorkshire in 1963. He has worked as a probation officer and more recently as the Poetry Editor at Chatto & Windus. His four collections of poetry are *Zoom!*, *Kid*, *Book of Matches* and most recently *The Dead Sea Poems*.

Gillian Clarke's most recent poetry collection is *The King of Britain's Daughter* (Carcanet). Her *Selected Poems* (Carcanet) were published in 1985. Born in 1937, she read English at the University College of Cardiff. After two years in London as a news researcher for the BBC, she returned to Wales in 1960. Now a freelance writer and teacher of creative writing, she has recently translated the *Mabinogion* for children.

Tony Curtis is Professor of Poetry at the University of Glamorgan. His most recent poetry collection, his seventh, is *War Voices*. He is the editor of several books, including *The Art of Seamus Heaney* (Seren).

Helen Dumore is a poet and novelist who has published six collections of poems, of which the most recent are *Recovering a Body* (Bloodaxe, 1994) and *Secrets*, a collection of poems for children (Bodley Head, 1994). Her poetry has received the Poetry Society's Alice Hunt Bartlett Award, the Signal Poetry Award and a Poetry Book Society Choice and Recommendation. Her novels include *Zennor in Darkness*, *Burning Bright* and *A Spell of Winter*, all from Viking Penguin. *Zennor in Darkness* won the McKitterick Prize, and *A Spell of Winter* won the Orange Prize; currently she teaches on the MA in Creative Writing at the University of Glamorgan.

Vicki Feaver was born in Nottingham in 1943. She has published two collections of poetry, *Close Relatives* (Secker, 1981) and *The Handless Maiden* (Cape, 1994). A selection of her work is also included in the new series of Penguin Modern Poets, Volume Two. She teaches at the Chichester Institute where she leads an MA in Creative Writing.

Lawrence Ferlinghetti was born in 1919 in New York, educated in
the States and at the Sorbonne where he was awarded his doctorate
in 1950. A major poetic voice in America since his debut as one of
the 'Beat Generation' in the 1950s, Ferlinghetti has also been one
of the most notable of poetry publishers through his City Lights
Bookstore and publishing house in San Francisco. Since 1955 he
has written over fifty collections of poetry, drama and fiction and
has been a mentor and role model for two generations of American
and British poets.

Michael Longley was born in Belfast in 1939, and educated at the
Royal Belfast Academical Institution and Trinty College, Dublin,
where he read Classics. For twenty years he worked for the Arts
Council of Northern Ireland and initiated the programmes for
literature and the traditional arts (mainly Irish music) and arts-in-
education. His early retirement at the end of March 1991 coincided
to the day with the publication of his first collection for twelve years,
Gorse Fires, which went on to win the Whitbread Prize for Poetry.
His *Poems 1963-1983* was re-issued the same year. A new collection,
The Ghost Orchid, was published in May 1995: a Poetry Book
Society Choice, it was also shortlisted for the T.S. Eliot Prize. He
has edited Louis MacNeice's *Selected Poems* and *Poems* by W.R.
Rodgers. In 1993 he was Writer Fellow at Trinity College Dublin.
A fellow of the Royal Society of Literature and a member of
Aosdana, he is also a founder member of the Cultural Traditions
Group which aims to encourage in Northern Ireland acceptance and
understanding of cultural diversity. He is married to the critic Edna
Longley, and they have three children.

Don Paterson was born in Dundee in 1963. He left Scotland in 1984
to work as a musician in London. He won an Eric Gregory Award
in 1990, and the Arvon/Observer poetry competion in 1994. His
first collection, *Nil Nil* (Faber) was a Poetry Book Society Choice,
and won the Forward Prize for Best First Collection and an SAC
book award. His second collection, *God's Gift to Women*, will be
published by Faber next year. He recently held the post of Writer-
in-Residence at Dundee University, and co-leads the jazz-folk ensemble
Lammas; their most recent recording is *The Broken Road* (EFZ).

Anne Stevenson, born in Britain of American parents and brought
up in the United States, presently divides her time between a small
cottage in Granchester and a farmhouse in Llanbedr, North Wales.

Her ten collections of poetry — most published by Oxford University Press — include *Correspondences* (1974), *The Fiction-Makers* (1985), and *Four and a Half Dancing Men* (1993). A frequent contributor to *Poetry Wales*, she is also the author of a number of controversial books and articles. A selection of her essays will appear in the Univsersity of Michigan *Poets on Poetry* series early in 1997. The full range of her *Collected Poems* is being published by OUP in England and America, to appear in mid September, 1996.

Acknowledgements

Acknowledgements are due to the following publishers for permission to reprint work by the following poets:
Dannie Abse: extracts from 'The Marriage' from *After Every Green Thing* (1948). 'Portrait of the Artist as a Middle-Aged Man' from *Funland and Other Poems* (1973), 'Epithalmion' from *White Coat, Purple Coat: Collected Poems 1948-1988* (1989), 'Cricket Ball' from *On The Evening Road* (1995). All published by Hutchinson, and reprinted by permission of Shiel Land Associates Ltd. **Simon Armitage**: 'Goalkeeper With A Cigarette' reprinted from *The Dead Sea Poems* (1995) by permission of Faber and Faber Ltd. **Gillian Clarke**: extracts from 'The King of Britain's Daughter', 'Llŷr' and 'The Stone' reprinted by permission of Carcancet Press Ltd from *The King of Britain's Daughter* (1995). **Helen Dunmore**: 'In the Desert Knowing Nothing' reprinted by permission of Bloodaxe Books from *Recovering a Body* (Bloodaxe Books, 1994). **T.S. Eliot**: extract from 'East Coker' reprinted from *Four Quartets* by permission of Faber and Faber Ltd and Harcourt Brace Jovanovich Inc. **Vicki Feaver**: 'The Lily Pond', 'Ironing' and 'The Handless Maiden' reprinted from *The Handless Maiden* (Cape, 1994) by permission of Random House UK Ltd. **Lawrence Ferlinghetti**: 'Uses of Poetry' and 'Poet as Fisherman' reprinted by permission of the poet. **Michael Longley**: 'The Thaw' and extracts from 'Ars Poetica' from *Poems 1963-1983* (Secker and Warburg, 1984) and 'Trade Winds' from *Gorse Fires* (Secker and Warburg, 1991) reprinted by permission of Reed Books. 'Chinese Whispers', 'She-Wolf' and extracts from 'Phemios & Medon' reprinted from *The Ghost Orchid* (Cape, 1995) by permission of Random House UK Ltd. **Don Paterson**: 'Candlebird' reprinted from the forthcoming *God's Gift to Women* (Faber, 1997) by permission of Faber & Faber Ltd. **Theodore Roethke**: 'My Papa's Waltz' reprinted from *Collected Poems* by permission of Faber & Faber Ltd and Bantam Doubleday Dell Publishing Group Inc. **Anne Stevenson**: 'Alas' and extracts from 'New York' and 'A Sepia Garden' reprinted from *Collected Poems* (1996) by permission of Oxford University Press.